Dear Folks

A FARM BOY LEAVES HOME TO FIGHT IN THE GREAT WAR AND FALLS IN LOVE WITH AN ENGLISH LASS

(Based on his actual letters home)

By
Walt Hazelton

Published in the United States of America

ISBN 979-8-89395-707-5 (SC)
ISBN 979-8-89395-706-8 (Ebook)

Library of Congress Control Number: 2024921826

Walt Hazelton Publishing
222 West 6th Street
Suite 400, San Pedro, CA, 90731
www.stellarliterary.com

Order Information and Rights Permission:

Quantity sales. Special discounts might be available on quantity purchases by corporations, associations, and others. For details, contact the publisher at the address above.

For Book Rights Adaptation and other Rights Permission. Call us at toll-free 1-888-945-8513 or send us an email at admin@stellarliterary.com.

Preface

As I was looking through old family documents I came across some letters my father had written to his parents while he was serving in the Canadian army during the Great War. These letters had been written 100 years before I found them and I soon discovered that they told a very interesting story of my father's life during that war. I decided to capture that story in this book.

I used the actual names of most of the people who are mentioned in this book so that my broader family and descendants can relate to the people that are mentioned. This may lead to some confusion, especially for my father, Walter, since his full name was Walter A. Hazelton, Jr. He was the son of Walter A. Hazelton, Sr. who was a doctor. Many of the letters that are captured in this book were written by Walter, Jr. to his parents whom he addressed as Pa Pa and Ma Ma.

Dr. Hazelton and his wife Minnie May Miller Hazelton had six children. The first three were born in the U.S. and the last three were born in Girvin, Saskatchewan, Canada. Specifically they were:

Helen: born in Baraboo, Wisc. in 1893

Walter: born in Baraboo, Wisc. in 1897

Ruth: born in Baraboo, Wisc. in 1900

Gladys: born in Girvin, Sask. in 1905

Florence: born in Girvin, Sask. in 1906

Louise: born in Girvin, Sask. in 1907

The story of Walter, Jr.'s life in the early 1900s begins with his childhood on a farm in rural Canada. It then transitions to his life in the Canadian Armed Forces, which includes his experiences in trench warfare primarily near the town of Ypres, Belgium. After being sent back to England to recover from some sickness he meets and subsequently gets engaged to an English girl. He also is accepted as a cadet in the R. A. F. and remains in England to train to be a flyer. The final chapters encompass the two years after the Armistice as he deals with the engagement to his English lover from a distance. He had been shipped back home and could not bring her with him on the troopship.

Walter's letters were written from the many places he found himself during those four years—including training camps, trenches, hospitals, his fiancee's home, hotels, etc. Whenever he got a chance to write he would use whatever scrap of paper that was available. Sometimes it was just plain notepaper but it also included Y.M.C.A. letterhead, military notepaper, business paper and hotel letterhead. To complicate matters more, he often had to write these letters in awkward conditions such as in a trench using his mess kit on his knee as a table.

Thus, this is a story of a young man experiencing the worst of mankind's horror with the fighting in the trenches and who then falls in love with an English lass he met while recovering in England. It paints a picture of his struggle with the changing moral codes in the places he finds himself in and how he regained the basic moral code that he was instilled with as a youngster.

This book also brings home the horrific conditions that existed in the trenches during that war. I, like most people, had no real appreciation of the horrors of that war. While trying to capture my father's experience I found it important to read a number of books that described war in detail. This allowed me to capture some of the specific situations around my father's experiences but also put them in perspective of the bigger picture.

Dear Folks

A farm boy leaves home to fight in the Great War and falls in love with an English lass

(Based on his actual letters home)

Contents

Chapter One
Growing Up

On November 4, 1897 Doctor and Mrs. Hazelton had a son who was given the name Walter, Jr. Walter, Sr. was a doctor with an office in Baraboo, Wisconsin which is a small town in the central part of that state. It was a beautiful place to live with abundant lakes and parks. However, winter could be a problem with frequent cold and damp spells. This caused some respiratory problems for both Walter and his father. This became a even bigger issue for Walter during the war but it also may have saved his life.

Because of the health problems Walter's father began looking for a place with a dryer climate He came upon an offer by the Federal government in Canada to give land to prospective farmers. This was the Dominion Lands Act which was enacted in 1872. The purpose of this legislation was to attract people to the sparsely populated North-West Territories.

The lands act provided 160 acres of undeveloped land to prospective farmers with only a ten dollar registration fee. The farmers had to live on the land and develop it during the first few years.

The Dominion government launched an intense advertising campaign in the Northeast of the United States to attract farmers. This seemed to work very well. Regina, Saskatchewan, the capital, had only 1000 residents in 1883 but tripled in size by 1900 and exploded to 193,000 by 1918. Saskatchewan Province[1] grew from 91,000 people in 1901 to 492,000 by 1911.

Dr. Hazelton became aware of this opportunity and decided it could be the answer to the health issues that he and Walter were experiencing in Wisconsin. So, in 1902 he took advantage of this offer and moved his family to the town of Girvin, Saskatchewan. It was a trip of over 1000 miles which in those days was not easy to do especially with a family of five and with all their belongings.

Girvin was a very small town with only a few hundred people. It was about 80 miles northwest of Regina so quite a distance to the closest town of any size.

Farming

Dr. Hazelton's move of the family to Saskatchewan definitely accomplished the goal of getting to a drier climate but it also resulted in much colder temperatures, sometimes as low as 49 degrees below zero Fahrenheit.

The farming itself also had it challenges with a very short growing season and frequent dry spells. During a 10 year period the Hazelton farm had only two good crops. Fortunately, Dr. Hazelton could earn money with basic medical services. However, many of the other farmers also had problems with their crops and sometimes they had to pay for their medical needs with goods instead of money. In one case, Dr Hazelton received a pig for payment.

During the harvest extra hands were needed to bring in what crops there were. Mechanical farm equipment was at its infancy which meant much of the work was done with horses or by hand. Often the older children were called upon to help with the easier tasks.

---

[1]Saskatchewan was designated a Province in 1905

Life on a Farm

During the first five years on the farm Dr. Hazelton and his wife had three more children, all girls. That brought the family to eight people. They all had to share a small farmhouse that had only three bedrooms. The five girls slept on big beds in two of the bedrooms, two on one bed and three on the other. Walter was the lucky one with a room to himself. Chores were given to all. Water had to be brought in from the well. Mother taught the older girls about cooking and sewing. And, they all helped with farm work as best they could. When Walter was in his teens he even learned to drive a tractor and shoot a gun.

Girvin, Saskatchewan was in an area that was largely a treeless prairie. The only trees were the ones planted by individual farmers. It was also very flat so you could see many miles in each direction. In the winter any blizzard had a long sweep and in the summer heat storms were violent. In such events the family held pillows against a large parlor window to keep it from blowing in. In the winter the snow drifts became very high. Once it was necessary to make a tunnel between the house and the barn. At times the snow became so hard the children could walk and play on the banks with no danger of it breaking through. Winter could also be a fun time for the kids. They rode to church in a big open sleigh padded with straw and hot bricks wrapped in newspaper to put their feet on. There was even one foot warmer for the mother and maybe someone else. It had a little drawer which pulled out so that charcoal pieces could be put into it. They were heated in the kitchen stove until they were glowing red. These charcoal bits stayed hot a long time and kept their feet warm until they got back home.

Saturday evenings everyone had to have a bath in the tub. They used a big copper boiler filled with water from the outdoor well. The bathing had to be divided up in order to provide for each person. They took turns bathing in the round galvanized wash tub.

The girls all had long hair so it was quite a job getting bathed and heads washed while keeping warm enough in the cold weather.

One of the bedrooms which was shared by two of the sisters sisters had a stovepipe coming up from the heater downstairs and it had what they called a "drum" in the portion going up through the bedroom floor which provided some heat in the bedroom. There were 6 kids. The oldest was 13 years older than the youngest so the older girl shared the other bedroom with the younger girls.

Horses were used extensively initially since tractors were rare. Eventually a large tractor was bought for plowing and threshing the grain etc. The farm was very large and it took extra help to do all the planting and harvesting so they had to hire temporary help during those times. A bunkhouse was available for the extra helpers. Of course they were not needed during the winter months but during the warm months there were many mouths to feed and many loaves of bread to bake.

It took a lot of food so there was a lot of canning to do. Potatoes and a few other vegetables were stored in the cool basement of the house or a "root cellar" which is a room dug in the ground and covered with sod so it would not freeze. Hundreds of jars of fruit and vegetables must be canned every year to provide for the winter food. Sauerkraut was made in a large barrel with pickles.

In spring all of the kids had to help with gardening. They learned to plant, weed, and harvest. On a farm everyone works almost as soon as could walk, certainly before they were old enough to go to school.

The school building itself was a challenge. It had one room and as many as 25 desks. Getting there was also a challenge. The six kids sometines shared a ride on the horse but more often they had to walk with their lunch bucket in hand. If anyone was late to school they were punished by having to sit in a big wooden box. There wasn't a furnace or central heating just a pot-bellied stove and a big wood box. It was very embarrassing to sit in the wood box right in the room with all the pupils watching.

They all learned to ride horseback on old "Jenny". She would stop dead in her tracks if she felt anyone slipping off her back. They herded cattle on old Jenny too and could almost lie down and go to sleep on her broad back. She was also used to round up the cows and drive them to the barn.

The barn was a fun place for the kids. They played in the hay and when the straw stack was high enough they could climb up to the pinnacle of the barn. Sometimes they dropped the cat out of the hayloft window to watch it always land on its feet, as they had been told it would do.

The kids could walk along country roads or roam the fields without fear or appreciation for what was going on in the rest of the world. Then the war broke out and things changed. They had no idea what war was All the young men in the neighborhood joined the service and only 3 of them ever came home again.

When the crops were ready to harvest it became a very busy time. The wheat was cut and then "stooked". In Canada you stand 2 shocks up on end together and the 2 more at their sides so they can dry out before threshing time. At the time of threshing all of the kids had jobs to do such as taking lunches to the farm hands out in the fields. Time was very precious during the harvest and the men couldn't stop and go all the way to the house for their noon meals.

There was a bunkhouse nearby where all the men slept. Sometimes there were quite a few. During the dry season they had to go by wagon and haul big wooden barrels to a spring some miles away to get water. That must have been a big job but the girls got to go along One day they got a frog in the water and took it out and fed it flies. That seemed like such a little thing but it was very exciting then.

There was no television or movies. However, there were barn dances for the older kids. Social life was very limited. Friends came for Sunday dinner and at Thanksgiving they sometimes rode over to a friend's house and had a nice dinner there. That was a big event.

The whole family went to church Sundays in a nice black phaeton, which is a buggy with a top and lamps on the fenders. Dad had bought the phaeton for mother and it was kept in the buggy shed. One day the son who was probably only 14 years old at the time decided to take the 3 little sisters for a ride, so he tied the horse to the back of the carriage and tried to get the horse to pull the carriage out backwards. Well he succeeded and after it was out a ways he decided to go forward and mother's new carriage went upside down with 3 little girls under it. None of them were hurt, but the pretty carriage was never the same. Walter never tried that trick again.

Walter tried another thing when he was about 14 or 15. He decided to shoot the rifle that was used for hunting purposes. He had heard about removing the powder from shells and changing it for some reason. Well, he went to a neighbor's field to try it out and the gun exploded and killed the neighbor's horse and burned Walter with powder burns. His father was away so the older sister had to clean and dress his powder wounds. That was another learning experience for a young boy.

Sunday was a very special day. Shoes must be cleaned Saturday so they were ready for church the next day. The kerosene stove was cleaned and the baking done on Saturday as well, since Sunday was a day of rest. That involved going to church in the morning and in the afternoon they would read the Sunday School paper and maybe play Bible Authors or things such as that but hey could not play boisterous games on Sunday. The father often read Bible stories to the three little girls as he held them on his lap with the arms of the big leather rocker holding them on. They loved to hear

Father read to them and if he came to a sad part or if the Holy Spirit blessed him he would almost cry. He was a very tender man and loved God dearly.

The grocery store was too far away to go often, so on a farm you only bought "staples" at a store and lived mostly on home canned and home baked food. Going to the store was rare and the three kids seldom got to go. But when they did go they were allowed to spend 5 or 10 cents on candy which was usually a penny a piece. It took a long time to decide what they wanted because they seldom had such a chance.

Ten out of the 14 years Walter, Sr lived in Canada he lost his crops by drought or hailstorms or some natural disaster, so by the end of 14 years he had to borrow money from his brother in Illinois to get out of Canada and back to Baraboo, Wisconsin to resume his medical profession.

The highlights of their young lives were the rides with Dad with the horse and wagon, and lying on the grass under the tree and watching the pretty, fleecy clouds. They loved to listen to Bible stories on Daddy's knee and prayers on Mama's knee. They also did family devotions with the deep love and understanding of a godly father and being taught honor and purity by both parents. They did not know they were poor because they were rich in many ways. Dad did not leave them \ riches like silver and gold or property, but he left them a very rich heritage of spiritual values and a deep conviction of the truth of God's word and His abiding presence and the assurance of eternal life through Jesus Christ, God's son.

A young Boy Grows Up

Walter's life growing up was certainly a challenge. His family of eight lived in a small farmhouse with no electricity and no running water so the day to day life could be difficult. However this also provided a number of learning experiences which would be very useful later in life.

The school was just one-room so a lot of the learning was done in stages. The teacher had to deal with all levels of learning by giving assignments to various grade levels to work on while teaching a specific topic to another level. But despite the many distractions all the children managed to get a very good education.

The strictness of the upbringing also prohibited drinking of alcohol, smoking, card playing, dancing and even the use of make-up for the girls. There were few opportunities to socialize with other children. However, Walter was good-looking and did manage to have a girlfriend even though that would have been done without much physical contact.

He was also busy helping his parents with all the chores around the farm including taking care of the animals. One aspect was protecting them from predators. For this Walter learned to use a gun. He quickly became a very good shot and would go after the prairie dogs as well as the larger pests. Before learning how to shoot a gun he had another way to get the prairie dogs. He would put a noose at the end of a long rope and put a stake in the ground of an active prairie dog hole. The noose would be looped over the stake and around the hole. He would then lie quietly nearby, wait for the prairie dog to emerge and then pull on the rope. If he was quick enough the prairie dog would be tied to the stake so Walter could then dispose of it.

Walter also was good at learning about mechanical things so when his father bought a tractor Walter was able to get an early appreciation of their operation. The tractor they had was given the name of Old Mike. His father also went in with some of the other nearby farmers to buy a harvester which Walter also took an interest in.

Early picture of the farm in Girvin

A picture of the farmhouse ten years later

Walter in front of the one-room schoolhouse

Old "Mike"

Many hands working the harvester

Chapter Two
Signing Up

At the beginning of summer in 1914 Walter had just finished his sophomore year in high school and the biggest concern for his father, as well as all the other farmers in the area, was the hope of having a good growing season. The weather extremes for the past number of years had resulted in poor harvests so that was first and foremost in their minds. The political turbulence in Europe certainly was not of concern to any of them.

This all changed on August 4 when the Germans suddenly invaded Belgium on their way to France. While many people were taken by surprise, it was not a surprise to the governments of most European countries. For instance, on August 2 Canada had already indicated they would provide a large force in the event war broke out. Even as early as 1839 the possibility of Germany using Belgium as an avenue for war was anticipated with the signing by England, France and Germany of a pact to keep Belgium neutral.

When Germany actually invaded Belgium, England immediately honored that pact by declaring war on Germany and Canada's position within the British Empire meant that it too was now at war with Germany. But Canada was not prepared to provide help immediately. Its permanent army had only 3000 people. There was no air force and only a couple ships in the navy. There did exist militias within the provinces with about 75,000 citizen soldiers but these had very limited training. Despite this, the Canadian government set a target of providing an Army of 25,000 to England which would be available as soon as formal training could be done.

At the same time the battles were continuing. It took Germany only a few weeks to march through Belgium despite heroic efforts by the out-manned and out-gunned Belgium army. Belgium was the only place along the French border that was suitable for an armed force to quickly move through due to its relatively level terrain. The German army was able to move relatively quick through this area considering their limited means of transporting troops and supplies. Meanwhile, the French and English armies continuously fought back until the German army reached the Marne river on September 6. The allies put up a very effective defense at this line. And since the German army had also outrun its supply lines it needed to pause.

To the north British forces also put up a successful defense in the area know as Flanders including the town of Ypres. This extended the allied defensive line from the Switzerland border to the Belgium coast. By the end of September both sides had dug in and the trench warfare, that would cause hundreds of thousands of casualties, began. These lines would exist for two years without changing by more than 10 miles in either direction.

While this was going on the Canadian government was moving forward with raising the army they had promised. One battalion was formed quickly with the financial help of a private citizen. It was made up of veterans from all parts of Canada. It was ready to sail within three weeks and left for England in December. With the limited amount of training needed they were also ready to leave England for France in late December and entered the line in early January. This force was named the Princess Patricias (nick named the Princess Pats) and would perform with distinction in upcoming battles.

In order to create the force of 25,000 that was promised a summons went out on August 6. There was no draft in place so they had to rely on volunteers. Canadians throughout the country jumped at the opportunity to sign up. Many were afraid they would miss out on the chance to get involved since most people were convinced that the war would only last a few months. Long lines quickly formed at the recruitment centers. Within a month there were so many volunteers the recruiting process had to be temporarily stopped. This first group of volunteers became the First Division. They were quickly organized into battalions. With limited training they were shipped out to England on October 2 where the real training would be provided. This lasted until early February at which time they were sent to the front.

With so many volunteers it was easy for the Canadians to create the Second Division just 3 days after the first was formed. Within these early volunteers there were many young men that Walter knew. He was just 16 years old and starting his junior year of high school. Even if he wanted to sign up with the others he would not be accepted at so young an age. So he continued his education and watched the events unfold in Europe especially as it involved the Canadian First and Second Divisions. They had been sent to the northern front in an area that became known as the Ypres Salient. This was a bulge in the line that protected the town of Ypres. Even though this was a difficult area to defend the Allies wanted to hold this part of the line to prevent the Germans from advancing along the coast.

There were a number of battles along this line that caused significant casualties for both sides. The first was the Battle of Ypres which was a month-long series of thrusts in October in which each side was trying to break through but with little success.

Then in March the Canadian First Division entered the line. It wasn't long before the 2nd Battle of Ypres occurred. The Canadians were in the line when, on April 22, the Germans unleashed Chlorine gas. It was a heavy gas that attacked the lungs and incapacitated anyone who breathed it. The use of gas in warfare was specifically prohibited by the Hague conventions of 1899 and 1906 so the Allies were caught off guard. The specific part of the line in which the gas was first released was to the left of the Canadians however some of it drifted into their area causing many casualties. Gas masks had not been invented so the toll was heavy in the parts of the line where the gas was released. Two French Divisions which received the worst of the gas were almost totally wiped out. The Canadians lost nearly half of their strength.

Many more battles continued through the spring and summer of that year. Both sides were taking heavy losses which needed to be replaced. Even though the Canadian government had already sent both the 1st and 2nd Divisions over in early 1915 they wanted to provide additional support so in December they started forming a 3rd Division. Volunteers had continued to pour in without regard to the news of all the losses. These men could not possibly be aware of the terrible conditions in the trenches. But the enthusiasm to join up persisted. This included Walter who in August of that year, at the age of 17, lied about his age and enlisted.

Here he was, a young naive farm boy who was raised in a household with the highest of moral standards. Suddenly he was going to be thrust into a world where standards of conduct were very different.

7-4-16

ATTESTATION PAPER.

No.

Folio 10 4312

CANADIAN OVER-SEAS EXPEDITIONARY FORCE.

QUESTIONS TO BE PUT BEFORE ATTESTATION.

	(ANSWERS)
1. What is your name?	Walter Arthur Hazelton
2. In what Town, Township or Parish, and in what Country were you born?	Baraboo Wis U S A
3. What is the name of your next-of-kin?	Walter A Hazelton (Father)
4. What is the address of your next-of-kin?	Edgeley Sask
5. What is the date of your birth?	August 4th 1897
6. What is your Trade or Calling?	Farmer
7. Are you married?	No
8. Are you willing to be vaccinated or re-vaccinated?	Yes
9. Do you now belong to the Active Militia?	No
10. Have you ever served in any Military Force? If so, state particulars of former Service.	No
11. Do you understand the nature and terms of your engagement?	Yes
12. Are you willing to be attested to serve in the CANADIAN OVER-SEAS EXPEDITIONARY FORCE?	Yes

Walter A Hazelton (Signature of Man.)

L Dingle (Signature of Witness.)

DECLARATION TO BE MADE BY MAN ON ATTESTATION.

I, Walter Arthur Hazelton, do solemnly declare that the above answers made by me to the above questions are true, and that I am willing to fulfil the engagements by me now made, and I hereby engage and agree to serve in the Canadian Over-Seas Expeditionary Force, and to be attached to any arm of the service therein, for the term of one year, or during the war now existing between Great Britain and Germany should that war last longer than one year, and for six months after the termination of that war provided His Majesty should so long require my services, or until legally discharged.

Walter A Hazelton (Signature of Recruit)

Date Sept 1st 1915. L Dingle (Signature of Witness)

OATH TO BE TAKEN BY MAN ON ATTESTATION.

I, Walter Arthur Hazelton, do make Oath, that I will be faithful and bear true Allegiance to His Majesty King George the Fifth, His Heirs and Successors, and that I will as in duty bound honestly and faithfully defend His Majesty, His Heirs and Successors, in Person, Crown and Dignity, against all enemies, and will observe and obey all orders of His Majesty, His Heirs and Successors, and of all the Generals and Officers set over me. So help me God.

Walter A Hazelton (Signature of Recruit)

Date Sept 1st 1915. L Dingle (Signature of Witness)

CERTIFICATE OF MAGISTRATE.

The Recruit above-named was cautioned by me that if he made any false answer to any of the above questions he would be liable to be punished as provided in the Army Act.

The above questions were then read to the Recruit in my presence.

I have taken care that he understands each question, and that his answer to each question has been duly entered as replied to, and the said Recruit has made and signed the declaration and taken the oath before me, at Regina this [illegible] day of [illegible] 1915.

(Signature of Justice)

Walter's enlistment document - he entered his birth date as 8/4/1897 which would make him 18 years old. His actual birth date was 11/4/1897 so he was actually only 17 when he signed up as shown on the expanded view on the next page

1. What is your name? .... Walter Arthur Hazelton

2. In what Town, Township or Parish, and in what Country were you born? .... Baraboo Wis U S A

3. What is the name of your next-of kin? .... Walter A Hazelton (Father)

4. What is the address of your next-of-kin? .... Edgeley Sask

5. What is the date of your birth? .... August 4th 1897

6. What is your Trade or Calling? .... Farmer

7. Are you married? .... No

8. Are you willing to be vaccinated or re-vaccinated? .... Yes

9. [illegible] .... No

On line 5 Walter entered his date of birth as August 4, 1897 but his actual date of birth was November 4, 1897

Chapter Three
Basic Training

As the grim fighting continued in Europe Walter began his military training. During the first few months preliminary training was conducted in Canada. This took about six months. So in March they were shipped to England for further training. The trip on a big ship had to be a little frightening for a youngster who had never before seen a large body of water much less an ocean. And if that wasn't enough the possibility of a submarine attack certainly had them all on edge.

Training in England was to continue until the boys were ready to go into battle. The first part was at the historic military camp at Shorncliffe which was in the southwest of England. It was here that he starting writing letters to his parents. The first of these is captured on the next few pages.

Risboro Camp,
Shorncliffe
Kent, Eng.
May 27, 1916.

Dear Father & Mother:

Well it is Sat. night once more. We have been at the Ranges everyday since last Sunday, but a new order says no more shooting on Sunday. We get up every morning at 2.30, go to the Ranges about 4.00. It is an hours walk. We carry packs. There is one

takes us to the foot of the Hill, about halfway

get another this coming

not nearly the class they are in Canada.

2 o'clock.

Some ~~so~~ didn't get

Risboro Camp
Shorncliffe
Kent, Eng
May 27, 1916

Dear Father & Mother:

Well, it is Sat. night once more. We have been at the Ranges every day since last Sunday, but a new order says no more shooting on Sunday. We get up every morning at 2:30, go to the ranges about 4:00. It is an hour's walk. We carry packs. There is one long hill and pretty steep. It is real hard climbing it when returning. The bunch comes back in time for dinner but we coaches have to stick to it about 2 hrs. longer putting Machine Gun men & signalers thro. I don't think very much of the job, but we have to do it if we can. You see, we shoot first every morning. Lots of times it is misty and sometimes the sun isn't up when we shoot. We don't have near the chance for a good score that those who shoot later have. But anyway I managed to get marksman's score. There's about a dozen in the Battalion got it. There are sixteen of us coaches, one for each target. We get the privilege of taking a bus if we pay our own fare. It takes us to the foot of the hill, about halfway home. The way things look we are going to be in for about a month of this work.

Tomorrow (Sunday) we move to another camp called Caesar's camp. It is supposed to be where Caesar had a Fortress. It is about another half hour's walk and up another hill, so we will be worse off than ever for the ranges. You won't need to change the address. It will get to me alright.

I have no idea when they will give us coaches leave, yet. It don't look any too promising to get any at all.

I had a letter from Helen & Ruth[2] but they hadn't got any of my cards & letters yet. It takes so long to get an answer to a letter that a fellow has forgotten when he wrote. About a month at least.

I haven't been able to go down town for some time now, because my uniform is worn out, but I expect to get another this coming week. I generally sleep in the afternoon anyway. But a fellow likes to be able to go down town when he gets a chance.

There has been no kick coming on the weather lately, it has been fine, excepting one day. Of course that had to come when we were on the 600 yd. range work. But we are lucky to have so little rain.

A new Commander took over our Battalion yesterday. Our old Officers have to go thru a training course.

The Range is at Hythe. Do you remember that piece in an Onward about the Crypt at Hythe containing so many skulls and Bones? Well, that is not from here. Some of the Boys have been to see it. I am going when I get some decent clothes.

I find that the common class of people here that we see most are not nearly the class they are in Canada.

In my opinion Canada has the Old Country skinned fifty ways in nearly everything. Things are more up to date & sensible over there.

As far as health goes I feel better here than I did in Canada but I still have my catarrh. A fellow often takes cold at night by having the blankets get off, but we get along O.K. I weighed myself at the beach a while ago on one of those slot machines and

[2]Two of his sisters

I weighed 153 so I have gained considerably. The food is not very palatable nor abundant but what we get is generally nourishing.

Do you know Eng. is on fast time? It changed the night before we went to the Ranges a week ago tonight. That same night there was an air raid over Dover (8 miles away) and lights went out early. We had to go out in Trenches and stay for a couple of hours, along about 12 o'clock. So we didn't get much sleep that night.

Verdun certainly is fierce isn't it. They are still doing their worst to get thru.

Well I guess I will have to go to bed.

How is business now? Are you all well? Remember me to my friends. How is Gladys getting along?

Hoping to get more word from across there soon.

I am as ever,
Your Loving Son,
Walter

Notice that in this letter, at a time in which the troops are getting ready to go into battle, Walter's tone seems almost upbeat. His lengthy description of the training program certainly did not convey any trepidation about the prospects of being injured or even killed when they actually got to the front. The troops were hearing news about the battles, especially Verdun, so it is surprising that there was no indication of any fear of the upcoming battles in this letter.

One of most interesting comments is his observation that the "*common class of people here that we see most are not nearly the class they are in Canada*". Walter was raised by devout parents, one of which was a doctor who was raised in a well-educated family. His mother also came from a successful family. So this very-well-brought-up kid is suddenly exposed to a different class of people. It may have been that the training camps were located in rural areas of England where the typical folks did not have the same opportunities he had. Or, that his upbringing in a "godly" home had set a pretty high moral standard for him. Clearly the differences were significant since he wrote about it very soon after arriving in England. This would become a problem in his subsequent, more intimate, relationship with a young English girl and her family.

In this first letter Walter also mentions becoming a coach on the shooting range. He was only eighteen at this point but his experience back on the farm shooting vermin certainly helped. In the first days of target practice he even got a marksman score which only a few could achieve. He certainly felt very good about that and it undoubtedly contributed to his seemingly high spirits.

It is also interesting that Walter would incur certain expenses even while at a training camp such as paying to ride the bus to the range. It turns out that he was having a significant portion of his pay automatically sent to his parents back home. He had not anticipated needing money for himself, thinking that the army would take care of his needs. After all, why would a soldier in the front lines need any money? In addition to the cost of the bus rides he would soon find that he also needed money when he got a few days off and could go into town. This was an important aspect of getting away from the training that many of the troops would eagerly take advantage of as long as they had money to do so. We will see that the money issue would recur throughout his time in Europe.

Walter also commented on his health being better. His father had moved the family from northern Wisconsin to the prairies of Saskatchewan for health reasons. Wisconsin had a damp climate that Walter's father wanted to get away from. Walter's health, however, would continue to cause problems later as he was subjected to the brutal life in the trenches. Also, during his basic training in Canada he must have lost weight, but had gained some of that weight back by this time so the camp food in England seemed to be good for him.

Walter in his private's uniform

Chapter Four
In the Trenches

Soon after writing the previous letter to his parents, Walter and his Battalion were shipped across the channel to the war zone. This had to be a scary time for him and his fellow soldiers. Up to now things had been very civilized but little did they know how chaotic and deadly it was actually going to be. Much has been written about how horrendous the trench warfare was and these optimistic young men were about to step into the thick of it.

****

Having just arrived on the continent and before actually getting to the front lines Walter took some time to write to his sisters:

June 26, 1916.

Dear Sisters & Bro:

Did you receive my last letter & handkerchiefs. I have had one letter from Papa & one from Jack's Mother since I left Eng. There must be a bunch someplace for me.

How are things going? What kind of weather are you having? I hope it isn't as wet as it is here. How are the cattle & crops?

Somewhere in Belgium

June 26, 1916

Dear Sisters & Bro:

Did you receive my last letter & handkerchief? I have had one letter from Papa & one from Jack's mother[3] since I left Eng. There must be a bunch someplace for me.

How are things going? What kind of weather are you having? I hope it isn't as wet as it is here. How are the cattle and crops? The other day we had a sports day and I met Ted Butler, Doust, Pat Blake, Ross Hart & that 46th bunch.[4] We beat them over after all. I haven't seen Jack Hornblin yet, but he is around here. I saw Jack Mathews. He and his chum are about the only ones left out of that first Qu'Appelle[5] bunch.

They are raising the deuce with the artillery lately, but we get used to it.

They have picture shows rigged up in sheds & old thatched roof barns, Y.M.C.A.s in every camp. You wouldn't think we were within range of Fritz's[6] guns.

I saw them bring down one of his planes the other day. Fritz sure had a long fall. We may go into the trenches any night now so if you don't hear from me for a while you will know everything is all right.

Remember in addressing just put name, no, 52 Battalion C. E. F. Army Post Office, London.

---

[3]Jack had married Walter's older sister, Helen, just six months earlier but his parents lived in England.
[4]These were some of his buddies from back home who had also signed up but were in a different unit
[5]Qu'Appelle is a town in Saskatchewan near where Walter grew up.
[6]Fritz was the common nickname for the German troops.

Well, I will have to quit for this time. I am writing on my mess tin & it isn't a very good table.

Hoping this finds you all as well as it bodes me. I am as ever

Your Loving Bro,

Walter

In this short letter to his sisters he seems to continue to have a positive view of his situation. He rather glibly mentions the sound of the guns and a German plane being shot down. There is no real concern expressed about being within range of "Fritz's guns."

But it wasn't long at all before he was to actually see battle.

By June of 1916 trench warfare had been in the typical battle front for just over a year. This was the case around the town of Ypres where units of the British Expeditionary Force (B.E.F.) were facing the German forces. Both sides had established complex trench defenses and had been attacking each other without much success. Typically a third of the Battalion would be in the trenches, a second part just to the rear as support trenches and the final group farther to the rear as a reserve in case of a German breakthrough. The men in the reserve might be able to have a good meal and a shower. Maybe even get some clean clothes. The three parts of the battalion would rotate about every six days.

Condition of the troops in the trenches after so many months of this type of fighting was wretched. Those in the front trenches, as well as the support trenches, would have no change of clothes or decent food for for nearly two weeks. Bathrooms were not available so a wing of the trench was used. If any of this group got killed they were stacked in another part of the trench.

The Allies decided that if they could mount a big offensive and push through the German lines the war might be over within a few months. Thus an attack called "the Big Push" was launched on July 1, 1916.

Unfortunately, the Allied command had overestimated what could be accomplished and underestimated how effective the German machine guns would be. Before the day was over almost 20,000 British men had been killed and almost twice that many put out of action, or captured, with very little accomplished. It was the bloodiest day in English history. As a result the Allies desperately needed to bring in reinforcements and Walter's unit was brought in the next day.

This is the situation that is described by Walter some years later:

It was June in 1916 and we were in camp at Shorncliffe[7], England getting our final training before going to the western front to help stem a German break thru and our 68th Battalion from Regina, Sask. was a part of the 3rd Expeditionary Force from Canada.

Rifle practice at the Hythe Range was in progress. I had done very well because I had used a rifle a great deal on the farm in Saskatchewan hunting coyotes and shooting gophers and so forth, so they decided I should coach on the range and show the fellows who were unaccustomed to rifles how to handle them correctly. (Incidentally a team of which I was a member won the championship of the British Empire and we were given a few days leave which I used to visit relatives of a friend of mine from home who lived near London.)

---

[7]Shorncliffe is a historic army training camp located southeast of London near Dover. It was originally established in 1794 and continued in operation until 2016. It was the primary training location for Canadian troops.

Due to a big German push in Belgium there were many casualties & reinforcement was needed so they decided to split up our 8th Battalion and send some of us to the "Princess Pats", some to the "Canadian Mounted Rifles" and others to the 52nd Battalion. We were asleep in our tents when the Sergeant Major came to awaken us and tell us which group we were assigned to, I was very disappointed when he said I was not included because I had not had my training in barbed wire and hand grenades. All of squad were going but me. We were all eager to get to the front before the war was over. I had resigned myself to staying behind when the Sergeant came back to say they were still short a few men and that I should dress and bring my rifle and "fall in". It was dawn by this time and as our names were called we fell in with groups according to the units we were assigned to. My name was called and I was told to fall in with the Princess Pats section, which I did.

Now, the rifle I had been issued was a "Ross". A long rifle with a short bayonet. The Princess Pats, however, used a short Lee-Enfield rifle with a long bayonet. The Sergeant Major brought us to attention and when his eyes caught sight of the long Ross rifle amid the short Lee-Enfields he yelled, "You with the Ross rifle, get over there with the other Rosses". So instead of changing rifles and leaving me with the Pats he crossed my name off his Princess Pats list and added me to the 52nd Battalion who had Ross rifles. Little did I realize how this incident was probably going to save my life because the Princess Pats were destined to be wiped out in the next few weeks.

By this time we were hearing how badly we were needed across the channel. After being issued the items we were short of we marched to a point of embarkation at Dover and were hurried aboard an old boat driven by paddle wheels. There was room to sit down and that was all. The channel was rough and if there were any that were not sick I did not see them.

I forget how long it was before we tied up at Le Havre, France. Hurriedly we were unloaded and immediately started on a march to a camp outside of Le Havre, where we camped and were to get some tough last minute drilling on the use of bayonets by some old line British Sergeant Majors. The Canadians resented this and could not understand why our Canadian Sergeant Majors could not do as well as the British. It was not long before each British Sergeant was joined by a Canadian Sergeant and everyone felt better.

They had found that the Colonial Troops, as we were called, resented being taken over by British for training. The next day we were loaded into little French box cars and were started for the front. After several hours we stopped and we knew we were getting closer to the front. The rumble we had been hearing in the distance was quite close now. We were at a place called Dicky Bush not far from the city of Ypres. The camp was all tents but very few troops were in sight because they were up in the front lines. That night they were relieved and they returned to camp. The Germans had been stopped but these men were in bad shape. The next morning was Sunday and we heard the famous author of "The Sky Pilot of No Man's Land", Ralph Connor, echo that the few who returned from the trenches had been through more than any troops in the History of war. They had been in the front lines three weeks steady and were thin, hollow-cheeked, and caked with mud from head to foot. We had begun to wonder why we had been so eager. That night, we who had just arrived were picked up to go out on a working party and try to clear out some communications trenches which were blown in by shell fire. These trenches were important because they were the only means of getting to and from the front lines without exposing the men to machine gun fire. It was hard work trying to shovel out the mud and we were glad when the time came, just before dawn, to get out of there. To reach these trenches we had come through the city of Ypres, which was in ruins. There had been three battles for the city and we were getting there at the end of the third. As we reached the gate, on the other side of the city, the continuous roar of artillery and the many "Veri" lights, which are star shells, could be heard and seen and we realized we were close to the front now. The city of Ypres was in a salient, it was surrounded on three sides by the trenches. This was known as the Ypres Salient, this was where we kids, I was eighteen then, were going with the few battle weary men who had been through so much. They had been sent out of the line just one day and were going back with us that night. I will never forget the looks they gave us as they wondered what good we would be when really under fire. The sector of the front line we were in had been held by the British troops until we relieved them. As we were led to the particular "bays" we were to take over, the Tommies moved out. Fortunately we were at the very point of the Salient and things were quiet excepting for a few star shells and bursts of machine gun fire from guns which had been sighted in on various points the night before. In each bay one man was always standing on the fire step which permitted him to look over the parapet and where he kept a sharp lookout for any attempt by the Germans to approach our trench. There was barbed wire out a few yards, placed in such a way that a few men could get thru it to points where listening posts were established in shell holes, usually. In the event of a sneak attack the listening posts would give the alarm. Before dawn, the listening post men would return to the trenches and look-outs would look over the top thru crude periscopes.

After getting acquainted with our surroundings, our officer selected some names for those who would be assigned to a listening post. Imagine my reaction when I was told I would go out in front on a listening post with two others who were old-timers. Well, when they found out I had just arrived they made some changes and took my name off the list. They thought I should have a little more experience before taking that kind of a job. Around noon that day things started up, the Germans started firing mortars at us. You could hear a thump in the distance and if you watched closely you could see a mortar coming your way. One at a time was not so bad because you could move to the next bay if it seemed too close but when several started out at the same time you could not judge where they would all land so you just hugged the side of the trench and hoped. Our first casualty came that day. One of the old timers got it right in the head.

I became very concerned about myself now. I was really scared and shaking. Was I really a coward? Then I noticed a couple of the old timers were shaking just as much as I was, and then I felt better. After that I became somewhat of a fatalist, but I prayed and read my little Bible as did many of the others.

Since we were in the point of the Salient no attempt was made to advance farther and we were there just to hold. The Germans seemed more or less satisfied to hold too. They had tried three times to take Ypres but overran it once and were driven back. So things were really quiet now except for around noon each day.

The second day they sent over a few high explosive shells which burst over the trenches and scattered shrapnel. I was hugging the front of the trench sitting on the fire step when one of the high explosives came right over. Afterwards I dropped my hand on something real hot and when I looked I saw a jagged piece of shrapnel half buried beside my knee in the timber there. That was the first of many close calls.

One of our group was not so lucky though. He got a piece in the leg and I was picked with one other man to carry him out on a stretcher that night. The stretcher did not have shoulder straps and it was very muddy from much rain. The load was heavy and we frequently slipped, jolting the wounded man who was in pain. It took us a long time to reach a dressing station where they gave us some cocoa before we returned to the front. The way back was a little different and it took us along a stretch of road known as "Dead Man's Corner". The Germans had machine guns trained on this road and had caught several who had tried to use it. Their bodies were lying there and the stench was awful. As we approached this stretch it was getting light so we decided to avoid it as much as possible even though it meant finding our way thru shells and mud. After we reached the Communications Trench it was less dangerous and we finally reached our outfit.

It was not until I was on duty watching for signs of German activity in no-man's land that I first handled a hand grenade, which we kept in pockets in the side of the trench. I was finally instructed in how to use them and told how the pin was pulled and the grenade thrown, not as a baseball, but with a stiff arm and overhand throw. Later, when we were back in reserve I had a chance to practice throwing them. If you wanted them to go off as soon as they hit the ground when the Germans were close, you pulled the pin and counted to 4 or 5 before throwing it. The grenade would explode in eight seconds from the time the pin was pulled. I was fortunate indeed that an occasion to actually use one did not come up for me.

The British had an old custom of giving their troops a tot of rum each day when they were in action or in the front line trenches. I had never tasted rum and when they handed me my ration the first time I was cold and wet and I eagerly gulped it down. Well,

I nearly strangled but it went right to my toes and warmed me up.

After a few days in the front lines we were relieved and moved back to the city of Ypres where we would be in reserve. Each squad was told to find a place to hole up. The city had been shelled so much hardly a building was standing but we found some wine cellars and underground rooms to stay in. Ours was a few steps down from what had been a beautiful courtyard with statues and figurines and a fountain.

The city of Ypres being surrounded on three sides by the front line trenches made it very unlikely that the Germans would use gas. At that time Chlorine Gas had been used some when the wind was right. It was released from cylinders and the wind would carry it to the enemy lines. Special squads were trained in its use but I was never present when our side used it. We all carried two gas masks which were chemically treated cloth hoods with two glass eye pieces and a valve for our mouths. We inhaled thru the nose and exhaled thru the mouth. In this way the air passed thru the chemically treated cloth before we inhaled it. The masks had a skirt which was tucked in under our tunic collars. We each had two in case the glass eye pieces were broken. The rules were that we were to carry them all the time and we were drilled in getting them out of the carrying cases and on in a hurry.

The Germans would need to have a wind blowing exactly right or the gas would blow right across to their own lines, so the danger of such an attack was practically nil and the rule of carrying the masks was rather lax for those quartered in Ypres.

Since we had little to do while there in the city some of us played cards.[8] It was a good way to pass the time and we played in one

[8]Apparently, by this time Walter had learned how to play cards since they were not allowed back home when he was growing up.

of the guards quarters. On this particular day I discovered that one of the eye pieces of my mask was cracked so I hung it up planning on getting a replacement as soon as I had a chance. We were playing cards when a clatter was heard and it continued for some minutes before someone realized it was a gas alarm. We all grabbed our masks and it was then that I discovered that I had hung up the good one instead of the one with the cracked glass. I had the cracked one and was worried. I hurried back to our cellar for the good mask and got it on just in time to save myself from the gas which drifted thru the city. There were a number of casualties among the mules which were tethered behind the batteries of artillery on the outskirts of the city, but no troops were caught except some in the front line.

Planes were now being used to spot enemy activities and just before dark the Germans sent a plane over the city, but there were anti-aircraft guns pom-pomming away trying to bring the plane down or keep it high. The plane would spot the gun and radio its position back to their artillery and then the shells started coming in. Those who were quartered near the ant-aircraft guns made themselves scarce but the boys firing the guns had to stick it out and hope they did not get it. The artillery was not very accurate and no one got hit that time.

Our next move was to the Somme Front in France. We were loaded in the little French box cars and traveled all night. Then we unloaded and marched all day thru a very pretty French countryside, stopping occasionally for rest. I remember that march particularly because the soles of my shoes wore thru and I was getting sore feet.

As we got nearer to the front lines, we camped that night in a wooded hilly area where we would be out of sight to any enemy planes that might come over. The next day I got new shoes and we marched some more until we approached the city of Albert, near the Somme River. Just outside of the city we stopped and made camp using our shelter halves. Each man carried one so in pairs we erected pup tents. Well it started raining again and it was soon a very muddy field, but if you had set up your pup tent correctly with a little ditch around it and had the edges covered with dirt you could lie inside without getting wet. That evening some of us walked into the city of Albert. It had been shelled but not nearly as badly as Ypres and some of the shops were open so we could get some fried eggs and bread. We had not seen eggs for some time and they tasted delicious. I also found a little shop that sold trinkets and souvenirs and bought a couple of pins which I later sent home to mother. The next day was Sunday and we were lined up in a formation to hear a chaplain but no sooner gathered than "Wham", a shell landed very close followed by a few more. It was rumored that some spy in Albert had managed to get word to the Germans' long range gunners that there was a concentration of troops, and exactly where. Needless to say, we were scattered in a hurry and only a couple were wounded.

That evening a long train of flat cars loaded with some large things covered with tarpaulins pulled up close to the city. We did not know it then but they were the very first tanks to be used in the war. The next day, September 15, they went into action.[9] They took the Germans by surprise and if there had been enough of them the war would probably have been over then. They advanced thru the line and the Germans retreated but the tanks could only go so far. They had to have supplies and gas which they had left far behind by now. Many tanks were crippled and were left stuck in the mud and the shell holes. We now learned that we were going to follow the tanks and try to keep the Germans on the run.

---

[9]These were the first tanks ever to be used in battle.

Our lieutenant at that time was a former school teacher from Saskatoon, Saskatchewan, a very likable young man and well liked by all of us. He now called us to all gather around and he drew lines in the dirt to show us where the Germans were and where we were going. It all looked so simple but this would be our first trip over the top and under direct fire.

We started out of the chalk pit in single file and after a little while came to a long slope where there were many shell holes. Here we were told to fan out and to fix bayonets. As we advanced I gripped my rifle so tight I was sure my fingers would leave imprints. I saw little spurts of dirt around us and I heard the whisper of bullets in the air. My best friend on my left slid into a shell hole and was fumbling in his tunic. He had been hit in the leg and was trying to get his iodine and field dressing which were fastened inside our tunics. That was the last I saw of him but he was one of the lucky ones because he would go back to a hospital when the stretcher bearers found him. The lieutenant was close by and he looked at me, gave me a wink, and motioned me to come on. In the distance machine guns were now getting the range but the Germans saw us coming with fixed bayonets and were running back not forward. They obviously thought we were coming right thru. When we came to a sunken road the lieutenant motioned us to stop there. Machine gun fire was heavy. He motioned us to keep down. Some of the men were slow in doing so and he stood up and yelled at them "For God's sake get down", as he was hit with a row of bullets across his chest. A sergeant told me to get the papers from his pocket and as I did so an order was passed along to fall back 50 yards and dig in! The German artillery had the exact range in the sunken road and were beginning to shell it. We fell back and lying on our stomachs got out our entrenching tools and started to scoop out a hole deep enough to lie in. You never saw entrenching tools working so hard and fast.

It was just getting dark and we had hardly finished digging-in when word came thru to move to the right where we learned that half of our men, all of our officers, and some of our non-commissioned officers had been hit.

A sergeant was taking command of the company. We also learned that a terrible error had occurred. It seems that just ahead was the famous Hindenburg Line. The night before, the Princess Pats had been ordered to take it. They had tried and had been repulsed. Orders had come that our company and another company were to try again to take it and that was where we were headed. Unknown to our officers and higher command, the Princess Pats had tried again and had succeeded this time, but that information had not arrived in time to stop the useless advance which had cost so many of our men. Of course, things like that happened in those days. Now, with walkie talkies and radios it would not. Then it was a case of sending messages by a wire strung along the ground or by runners.

Next we learned that we would move up to the Hindenburg line that night and relieve the Princess Pats. Of course, the Germans had the exact range on their old Hindenburg line also, so when we arrived and three volunteers were asked to man a listening post a few yards in front, two others and myself volunteered to take the job. Actually we believed it would be better than being in the main trench.

The famous Hindenburg line was very well built. It was deep, well-supported by timbers, and had good deep dugouts, which could be used if shell fire got bad. However that is one of the reasons it was taken later. Tactics had changed and a barrage of shell fire was laid down on the trenches and our troops had been instructed *and trained to follow the barrage so closely that the Germans would not be out of the dugouts before hand-grenades were thrown in. I was glad that I had not been with the Princess Pats whose job it was to do this.*

Since the back of the Hindenburg Line was now in front of us, there was no barbed wire there yet and it fell to the lot of those taking over to put out barbed wire and to bury as many dead as possible, and there were many.

We found our little outpost had a dugout which was a fairly good sized place to rest. Lying dead in the dugout was a German boy no older than myself. He had in his pocket a German Bible and a silver spoon with the kaisers head engraved on it.

The real facts of war were beginning to affect my thinking. If the ones who decided to make war had to do the dirty work and go thru the hardships and suffer as the front line troops had to, there would be no more war.

We took our turns at look-out and resting but our rations were gone. We heard that the ration party who was to have brought them up to us, had been hit and did not make it. So we ate our emergency rations which consisted of hard tack, tea and sugar. They were fastened inside of our tunics and were not to be used until we got the OK to do so. Our water bottles were filled with water and lime juice. It did not taste good so you drank it sparingly, but the lime juice was a good thirst quencher.

I recall one incident while we were in this outpost could have been fatal. The men standing on the lookout at night in the main trench were of course behind us and had been warned to be careful if they fired in our direction. On one occasion when I was on lookout and one of the other two was throwing something over the back of our outpost, the man on watch behind us saw movement and fired at us. Luckily he did not hit anything, but we were plenty sore about it and one of the fellows crawled back to the main trench to give them H. To his consternation it was not our company back there. They had been relieved and had left without telling the fellows who took their place that we were out there. Whoever was supposed to tell us the company was leaving had failed to do so and we were left behind.

Well, we did not know exactly where we would find them but we made our way to the rear that night, asking when we got a chance which way they went. After a while we found a deserted shallow cave and someone had left some bully beef, bread and jam so we ate and went to sleep. In the morning we found our way to the base camp in the chalk pits and decided to wait there for our company, but a new lieutenant was there heading for our unit also. He was to replace the school teacher killed a few days before. A guide was found to lead the lieutenant and ourselves out to a section of trenches where our company was in support and was badly in need of some supplies and food. I was a rather slim kid so the others volunteered to carry the supplies if I would carry their rifles.

It was daylight when we started but the runner did not seem too sure of the way. The guide was leading, the lieutenant followed him, and then two others with me bringing up the rear. The terrain was getting pretty rough and we came to an old trench which he thought was leading in the right direction so we followed it. Shells had blown in the side of the trench in places so there were gaps. At one of these gaps the guide passed and as the officer was passing by "crack", a sniper's bullet hit him in the leg. The next man passed the gap, "crack" again, but he was unhurt. The third man hurried across and was OK. Now here I was with three rifles knowing a sniper was going to try and get me. I thought he would figure we were coming at regular intervals and would time his shot accordingly so I threw the rifles over, waited *a moment, "crack" came the shot and then I hurried across the opening. Believe me my heart was in my mouth. We then decided not to proceed any further until dark and then take the wounded officer out. We bandaged his leg and he could walk with help. There was an old dugout in the trench so we decided to wait there while the guide went back to tell them what happened and then come back with more help. We never saw the guide again, however, so the two of us helped the officer back that night and the other fellow went on with as many supplies as he could carry.*

Later we learned that our guide had mistaken the path and had actually led us thru a gap in the front line and we were in no-man's land when the sniper spotted us. The lucky lieutenant went back to the hospital before he ever got to the front lines.

Canadian troops leave their trenches and head over the top at the battle of the Somme.
Robert Hunt Collection/Mary Evans

And below is another recount of one of Walter's experiences in the front lines:

A seemingly harmless act can sometimes prove a disaster.

Excepting for an occasional Flare everything was quiet on our sector of the Western front and both the Germans & ourselves were happy to keep it that way. We were in trenches at the point of a salient which had pushed beyond the city of Ypres, Belgium. There was no point in pushing forward until the line was straightened out on both sides of us. Our unit was the 52nd Battalion of Canadian Infantry & our orders were to not fire a rifle until ordered to do so· The third Battle of Ypres was ending after the enemy had occupied Ypres & were driven back· I was one of a group of re-enforcements rushed over from England to replace the many casualties from the last Battle· The men we joined in the 52nd had been thru Hell & they, understandably, were very disappointed to see a number of us who were so young and had not as yet been under fire· I was eighteen at the time & scared to death·

We took turns looking over the parapet & watching for enemy movement· Crude periscopes enabled us to do this in daytime without raising our heads over the top of the trench· At night the periscopes were no good so we had to raise our heads just enough to look over· The German Trenches were about two hundred yards away at this point·

Trenches were dug in a series of Bays so that if the enemy troops did get in they would not be able to direct their rifle and machine gun fire along the trench·

Well, all was quiet this July 4th night in 1916· I was on duty peering over the top of the trench & listening for any tell-tale noises which could mean a German raiding party trying to cut their way thru the Barbed-wire which was out in front a few yards· It was very dark that night & I had been standing there on the fire step for some time when two little points of light moved along the sand bags and stopped in front of my nose· I was startled until I realized it was a large rat looking me over & the first inclination was to raise my rifle and shoot it but I remembered the orders in time & let it proceed along to the next Bay· Well the boy standing watch there did not remember and bang went his rifle· Instantly everyone was alert· Star shells went up from both our trenches & from the German lines· Someone imagined they saw movement in the barbed wire & threw a hand grenade which was followed by several more· Heavy Machine Guns opened up where the grenades had exploded. By this time the Germans evidently thought we were starting something so Machine Guns that were zeroed in on our trenches before dark, opened fire also. No-man's land was lit up by many star shells now. No one was in sight but of course the shell holes out there provided places to keep out of sight. Even if they were out there in the open and stood perfectly still they would probably not be distinguished.

By this time someone had been on the field telephone & called back to the Artillery to join in & they began dropping shells on the German trenches. I guess they figured men were coming over the top on a raid because they immediately opened up with their Artillery and the entire area was ablaze. There were a number of direct hits on our trenches & a number of casualties resulted before it was realized it was all a mistake and things quieted down again.

I never did find out exactly who fired that first shot but you may be sure he was on the carpet for it. It just goes to show how some thoughtless incident can result in disaster.

Each day the Germans had made a habit of trying to locate our trenches with a few Trench Mortar Shells. We would hear a distant thud & if we watched closely we would see the mortar arcing toward us, and if we judged fairly accurately where it would land we could scoot into the next Bay, but sometimes they sent several at a time & we would just have to hug the front side of the trench & hope.

Life in the trenches was miserable and adding to that was the mortars. They were launched at a high angle so that when they came down they could land in the trenches. It was very difficult to find a safe place to hid from them. Walter had been shaken by the mortar fire more than once but when he saw that some of the old-timers were also having problems he was able to accept that when his time came, it came, and that was it. This allowed him to develop a state of mind to be able to deal with the perils of this terrible warfare without breaking.

Another problem was the threat of a gas attack. However, by this time the allies had made gas masks for the soldiers to have available but they didn't take away the scary aspect of this type of warfare. Walter had a few close calls.

Another problem in the trenches was how muddy they were with water often up to a soldier's knees. Those in the front lines were not able to get dry socks and shoes until they were relieved and returned to the recovery area which might not happen for several weeks at a time. This problem often caused terrible foot sores which became known as "trench foot".

One interesting development while Walter was near the front was his sighting of some mysterious items being brought in by train. They didn't know they were seeing the very first tanks.

Tanks

With the terrible losses experienced in the early stages of the war due to the effectiveness of the German machine guns the allies realized they needed to find a weapon that could negotiate the wire barriers without incurring massive manpower losses. The concept for such a devise had already been proposed by an officer of the Royal Engineers but was initially rejected by the war office. With the losses growing in early 1915 the proposed vehicle was given approval in the fall of 1915. After a successful trial in February of 1916 an order for 100 of the so called "land-cruisers" was placed. It was important to keep this a secret so a non descriptive name was needed. The word "tank" was decided because these large ugly things looked like storage tanks that were often found on farms.

The first use of the tanks was on September 15, 1916 when 49 were included as part of the battle of the Somme which included the Ypres salient. The attack started off well. The front line of the German army was overrun in 15 minutes with many of the soldiers running in fear. However, most of the tanks were soon put out of action, either because they could not handle the terrain due to the many bomb craters, or they ran out of gas.

The allies were so anxious to put the tanks into action they had started with too few of them. This gave the Germans an idea of what they were so that their army was soon able to provide a better defense against them. Having seen these monsters the Germans quickly started to make some of their own and thus began the era of tank warfare which became a big part of World War II.

The Battle of the Somme, which was kicked off on July 1, continued until September but most of the fighting was south of where Walter's battalion was located. During this time he got very sick and was sent to back to England to recover. Once he was better he was returned to his unit and had to deal with the horrendous trench like. The following letter was written after he had been in the front lines for a number of weeks:

(Letter 4)

On Active Service

Y.M.C.A.

WITH THE BRITISH EXPEDITIONARY FORCE

Somewhere in France

Sept. 26, 1916.

Dear Folks:

I know you will be waiting for this letter as it has been so long since I could write. But I hope you got the field cards & letter [illegible] neither get mail nor send any for quite a while. I received your letter dated Aug 26. the other day. But have not received Mama's parcel yet. It is a

I am still in the game.

A small percentage are

too busy. like flies in the sky,

I could have gotten German

my friends, who are

From somewhere in France

Sept 26, 1916

Dear Folks:

I know you will be waiting for this letter as it has been so long since I could write. But I hope you got the field cards & didn't worry.[10] *We could neither get more nor send any for quite a while. I received your letter dated Aug. 26 the other day. But have not received Ma Ma's parcel yet. It is a shame that the best one of all should miss carry. But perhaps it got broken. How was it packed? Boxes and tins nearly always get here to the boys but cardboard nearly always gets broken. I may get it yet. It may have been sent back to Eng. while I was sick. Next time if you can find two or three handkerchiefs to put them in. A small pair of scissors, folding if possible, would be real handy. One pair of socks (heavy) always comes in handy especially when we are doing a lot of marching as we are now.*

I am in the (first aid) section now. Stretcher Bearers, they are called. I have not done any work in the field with them yet. But will soon undoubtedly. Sometimes Fritz respects the Red Cross while they are bringing in the wounded & sometimes they don't. We have been in a hot scrap here, but I am still in the game. A small percentage are killed.[11]

It is nothing at all to take Fritz's trenches once they are reached. He either runs or throws up his hands. They seem only too willing to be taken prisoners. But he has quite a few machine guns which

---

[10] The troops were given picture postcards they could send back home. A few of these are included elsewhere is this book.

[11] Trench raids continued all through the war when there wasn't a major battle going on. However, even when they captured an enemy trench it was soon recaptured because it was built to defend the other way.

are hard to face & considerable artillery which he brings on his own trench as soon as we have captured it.

We made a charge & gained our objective & are out for a few days. Then we will go in again. I have seen more in the last ten days than I ever want to see again.

We are all earnestly hoping and praying that it will be over before winter & it quite possibly may be, but again it may not be. It is just a question of time now. They are giving it to him all along the line now. I saw several of his balloons burnt the other day. He can't get very good observation now. Our planes are too busy. Like flies in the sky.

Yes, I would be glad to have you write to Winnie[12] *once in a while. I know she wants to hear from you.*

I got a letter from Ruth & Helen[13] *the other day too. Ruth talked as if she expected to go to the States soon.*

Yes, I told you about me getting the cheque but in case you didn't get the letter, I got it cashed thro' the Y.M.C.A. captain. I bought a pretty good watch & several other things[14] *But that is too much anyway. A fellow spends it before he realizes it. If I could get from say 3 to 5 dollars a month it would be enough & yet be awful handy when a fellow comes out of the trenches. In some places they soak us fellows pretty bad especially if they think we have any money. A fellow can get any amount of souvenirs of any description but nobody is willing to pack them around. I could have gotten German rifles, bayonets, helmets, coats & everything*

---

[12] Winnie was his girlfriend before he left for the war

[13] His sister Ruth had stayed behind in Canada to live with her sister, Helen and her new husband when Dr. Hazelton moved the rest of the Family back to Haywood. Wisconsib.

[14] Apparently he wasn't too short of money at this point but he would be later.

in a trench we chased them out of. But we have all we can carry without extras. I have a German Bible or prayer book I am keeping.

I don't think anything in this world will ever be appreciated & welcomed as much as the end of this war. A fellow, no matter who he is, can never realize or even imagine what this war is like till he has been thru it for himself.

Say, can you get camphor bags or anything that will keep vermin away. You can't imagine how thick they are here.

Did Winnie tell you that Harry was in the Hospital. He is in the Truck Transport. If I had not have gone with that 1st draft I would have been too. But there is practically no chance of transferring now.

Well, I think that is all. I hope you can read this, but I am sure out of Practice now.

Remember me to all my friends, who are kind enough to inquire about me. I hope to see you all before a great while.

I think as you suggest, to come & finish H.S. then go in with you & gradually get into it myself is the best. I don't think there is a better profession than medicine or Osteopathy.

Well, I hope this finds you all well & happy.

I am your trusting & Loving

Son, Walter

Rte W. A. Hazelton #104312

What street do you live on & no.

A very telling comment in this letter is about the horror of what was going on: " *I have seen more in the last ten days than I ever want to see again"*. Other books have described the obstacles these men were facing and it is amazing that Walter could write about it at all. The one thing that probably kept him going was the hope of the war ending soon. It was just August of 1916 and the men were expecting it would be over by the end of the year.

This letter also reveals some of the hardships of life in the trenches including the lack of basic items. Some packages from home were getting through so Walter was hoping to get some things like handkerchiefs, a pair of scissors and some heavy socks. Also, something to repel the rats in the trenches which was just one more of the many hardships these soldiers were facing.

He was thankful for some money that was sent to him from home. Not surprising that the locals would "soak" them. However, he did buy a nice watch.

And, Walter was thinking ahead about his future. He had not finished high school so recognized he would need to do so. And he might want to follow his father into the field of medicine. (We will see that this was a short term consideration.)

There is also something interesting about this letter in that it is the first one where he signed it with "Your Trusting & Loving Son". Probably the word trusting meant trusting in the Lord to pull him through.

Chapter Five
Recuperation

Sometime after the previous letter was written Walter was sent back to England. The doctors had noticed some irregularity in his heartbeat[15] and thought this had better be resolved before putting Walter back in the trenches. This probably saved his life because the casualty rate for the troops in the trenches was going to be horrific for another two years.

There were no letters from Walter for some time but it seems that he got well enough to be able to go into town and visit with friends and relatives.

At some point while in town he became acquainted with a local girl named Cecile. Keep in mind the rather controlled home life that he had been raised in with no dancing, drinking, or card playing. So here he is in a rural English town where most of the local boys have gone off to the war. The number that were still around for the local girls to date had to be quite limited. And, for many of these girls, getting to know a soldier had to be very

[15] this heart irregularity was actually extra beats which actually are not a serious condition but doctors then did not understand it. Walter had them all through his life without any issues.

exciting, especially if he were good looking, well mannered, and from as far away as Canada.

During these months of recuperation Walter got to know Cecile quite well and had spent some time at her home. It was not unusual for soldiers to find a home away from home when they were in England. There weren't any letters, or at least any that were saved, to describe how he and Cecile met and how often they got together. Even though Walter was recuperating he must have been able to get away enough for this friendship to develop. The next letter home describes what had been going on:

For God, For King & For Country.

Y·M·C·A
H.M. FORCES ON ACTIVE SERVICE

Y.M.C.A. Y.M.C.A.

PATRON: Y.M.C.A. NATIONAL COUNCIL, H.M. THE KING. PATRON: MILITARY CAMP DEPT. H.R.H. DUKE OF CONNAUGHT.

Reply to ~~No 8~~ Company .... Bat. .... Regt. Jan. 19 1917
~~Stationed at~~ No 8 Platoon
No 2 Company.
C. Division,
C. C. Depot.
St. Leonards On Sea
Sussex,
Eng.

Dear Folks:

Well, I have had my ten days at last. I meant to write while at Mrs. Walkers, but didnt. I had a pretty good time. I first went to Uxbridge for a couple days & then to Liverpool. You see I told Mrs. Walker to write to Uxbridge in care of my chum there, if it was alright ~~to~~ for me to go on. I thought

must have been having

She has been working

the way.

Y. M. C. A.
Jan. 19, 1917
No 8 Platoon,
No 2 Company,
C. Division,
C. C. Depot
St. Leonards On Sea,
Sussex,
Eng.

Dear Folks:

Well, I have had my ten days at last. I meant to write while at Mrs. Walker's but didn't. I had a pretty good time. I first went to Uxbridge for a couple days and then to Liverpool. You see I told Mrs. Walker to write to Uxbridge in care of my chum[16] there if it was alright for me to go on. I thought she was still in Wales until the letter came, telling me to go to Liverpool. I went up there on Tuesday & then came back to Barnett (Hawkins) Friday mid-night. Then Monday morning I went back to Uxbridge again. I had figured out that Wed. was the 16th & not until Wed. night did I discover my mistake. That made me a day late & then I missed the last train that night. But the transport Officer wrote on my pass that I missed it on account of the numerous changes since the first of the year, so that was alright. But the day late wasn't alright & of course I was up before the O. C[17] when I got back. I told him I had no reason but had merely mistaken the date. That was certainly no excuse at all so he couldn't overlook it entirely. Consequently he let me off as easy as he could & that was 2 day C. B[18] & two day pay stopped. I finish my C. B. tonight at 9. But I have put my first crime on my Conduct sheet.

---

[16]The "chum" in Uxbridge was his new girlfriend Cecile.

[17] Officer in Charge

[18] Confined to Base

The O. C. said I must have been having an awful good time to miss a day like that. It certainly was some blunder.

When I got to Uxbridge I found that my friend's bro' had died. He had only been called up three weeks before. I saw him at Xmas & he died on New Year's day. They said it was heart failure but not in my opinion. They vaccinated & inoculated him on the same day and then he walked about 30 miles to get home for Xmas. I think it was that that did it. Then the Gov. would not have to stand any of the expenses as his mother wanted him buried at home. The father was sick and couldn't get home & his bro' could not get home from France, so just his sister and Mother, besides a few relations, could see him buried. That is two boys who have died in that family within a few months. It has affected his mother so bad she will have to go under an operation. I don't know what poor Cecile will do if they break up the home now. She has been working in a high class photographers tinting pictures & painting post cards. If the ones I have just taken are worth it, she will tint one to send to you. If you would like one I will try to get one of herself & send to you. I know you would like her, I don't see how anyone could help but like her & I never met a nicer old lady than her mother but she is not very old either tho' she looks it thro' having so much trouble lately. They have certainly given me a good time & made me feel right at home at their place.

I guess I didn't mention that I was inoculated yesterday, believe me I have a sore arm. But it ought to be getting better tomorrow. It releases me from duty for 48 hrs. so I have not had to do anything but report once in a while.

I received an Xmas box today from the Meth. Ladies aid in Appelle. It was very good & not much the worse for having been so long on the way.

Yesterday I had a letter from L. Jackson & one from Helen & Jack, both were written in Nov. I have not got any from you since I left Uxbridge, but I suppose if I am here long enough I will get them.

I have not seen Dr. Wickware for 3 weeks, but mean to hunt him up on Sunday.

I had a nice quiet time & rest at Mrs. Walkers. She is all alone & is trying to do the work herself. One night she and Miss Walker & myself went to a theater. It was very good too. I was not there long enough to meet many of their friends & Derrick had just left to take his Officer's training course in Ireland, so I didn't see him either. I think Mrs. Walker is a very nice old lady but she certainly ought not to live there all alone. I was sorry I didn't meet Derrick as I am sure I would like him.

Well how is everybody anyway? How is business? I have hardly written to anyone lately. It will keep me busy to catch up again.

I hope a few of your letters come along pretty soon. I am anxious to know how everybody is?

I am not feeling very well lately. The pains still bother me in the chest. If they do not let up I will report sick again. I wouldn't be surprised to see myself back in Hospital again before long. If I do, I certainly will not be sent to France again. We figure on the War to end sometime this summer.

Bye Bye for this time. Hoping this finds you all well & happy.

I am as ever,

Your loving & Trusting

son, Walter

By this time Walter had become very familiar with Cecile's family and was spending a lot of time with them and they were making him feel right at home. This relationship with Cecile would continue to develop into a more serious relationship over the next few months.

Once again in this letter we see the optimism about the war ending soon.

Walter's health continued to bother him as he commented about feeling sick again. Remember that Dr. Hazelton had moved the whole family from northern Wisconsin to the plains of Canada for his own health as well as Walter's so the health issue seems to be continuing.

It seems that Dr. Hazelton had contacted the authorities about Walter's health and he received the following letter from one of the doctors:

Jan 28/17

Dear W. Hazelton,

No doubt you will be surprised to hear from me but I have seen your son Walter recently. I wanted to tell you how well he looks and what a fine Chap. To tell you the truth I think he is home sick but is no shirker nor has the war game spoiled him. He is a fine clean cut boy that a father might justly be proud of and if he has any bad habits I fail to see them. You ought to see the way he prizes his letters from home.

At present he is at the Command Depot but am doubtful if he stands the training as he was never intended for a rugged but there is no sign of any Chest Trouble. If he gets through this war game safe he will be the happiest boy to get home. We are sick of the game but having put our hand to the plow we want a peace that will be lasting without a half hearted thing and now that we are ready to fight we want no interference. Already the Hun is Crying enough and we intend to wreak him. At no stage of the game have I seen our soldiers so confident. And the recent ones from the front are even more so. Now I am getting into talking war and the censor may stop this.

Don't think your boy is chickenhearted. He has a man's spirit in a boy's frame. Am glad to hear you are in practice again and doing well. Kind regards to Mrs. H. and family.

Yours truly,

JW Wickware

Capt. C.A.M.C

P.S. We had Walter to dinner with us

This letter was certainly welcomed by Walter's parents as it might have seemed to them that Walter's health was a big problem especially especially since he had been in and out of trenches several times.

*****

Walter's next letter was written from a hospital:

May, 2nd 1917.

Isolation Hospital
Highland Lodge.
St. Leonards-On-Sea.
Sussex, Eng.

Dear Folks:

Well I am having quite a time with the mumps. I have been real sick for several days. I couldn't keep any thing on my stomach & I had a bad headache all the time beside a fever. But the M.O. has not been near us for 4 days so we must get better the best we can. However I am feeling better tho' I am very week yet. This is just an isolated house practically, there are no hospital accomodations. They bring us our grub & what we need & that is about all there is to it. Measles have part of the House, Mumps are a room, & etc.

I received Papa's welcome letter of the Apr. 6th & was very glad to get it. Yes Helen & Jack ought to make something this year the way prices are. I haven't heard from them for some time. I had a letter from Winnie dated Feb. & she was at Qu'Appelle on a visit. She had evidently

May 2nd, 1917
Isolation Hospital
Highland Lodge
St.Leonards-On-Sea
Sussex, Eng

Dear Folks:

Well, I am having quite a time with the mumps. I have been real sick for a couple days. I couldn't keep anything on my stomach & I had a bad headache all the time besides a fever. But the Dr. O. has not been near us for 4 days so we must get better the best we can. However I am feeling better tho I am very weak yet. This is just an isolated house practically. There are no hospital accommodations. They bring us our grub & what we need & that is about all there is to it. Measles have part of the house, mumps a room, & etc.

I received Papa's welcome letter of Apr 6th & was very glad to get it. Yes Helen & Jack[19] ought to make something this year the way prices are. I haven't heard from them for some time. I had a letter from Minnie dated Feb. 1 & she was at Qu'Appelle on a visit. She had evidently ...

(page 2 of this letter is missing)

It was read to us from "Orders" today that we need not put stamps on letters to any Allied countries now. I wonder if that means U.S. too[20] It ought to. Of course we must use them on all English mail.

[19]Helen & Jack were trying to make a go of it in farming but there were not many good years.
20

I am glad you are getting along alright & sure hope it continues.

I am beginning to wonder when this war is going to end. Those Subs seem very much alive. I hope U.S. will send some men over soon. It ought to help a lot.

I am making a lot of mistakes in this letter but I am writing it in bed and besides I don't feel up to much. I have had a heavy aching in my chest a great deal since I have been in bed. I don't know what it is.

Well, I hope you are all well.

With love to All, I am always Your Hoping & Trusting Son.

Walter

P.S. I can't write a good letter today.

The hospitals and the doctors in England had to be overwhelmed with all the casualties that were streaming back from the battlefields. Clearly they could not dote on those with minor maladies, such as the mumps. So Walter, along with the others like him, were placed in isolation "hospitals" to recover. Walter seemed to be making the best of it and at least was able to write home to tell about it.

Also of note in this letter is the lack of hope that the war was going to end soon. He was hoping the U.S., which had declared war on Germany just a few months earlier, would send some men over soon. The men in the hospital were getting news about what was going on as we can see from his comment about the subs being very active.

Chapter Six
The Engagement

Several weeks after the previous letter was written, Walter was well enough to be released from the isolation hospital and had time to visit Cecile and her mother. He was fortunate to have this home away from home whenever he had a chance to go there. This next letter was written from their home which was called "Ernest Villa."

"Ernest Villa."
Cawley Mill Rd.,
Uxbridge, Mdx.
Eng.
May 23rd. 1917.

Dear Folks:

When I arrived here I found two or three letters awaiting me. One from Pa Pa. One from Ma Ma with clippings, & I enjoyed reading them believe me. It seems good to know what ~~kno~~ news you folks are getting. I also got Ruthie & Louise's letters & thanks very much for same.

I fully appreciate Pa Pa's advice, in answer to my special question. I realize it will be a hard fight to get a start in what ever work I decide upon. But whatever it may be, I am going to make good at it. I have a new, & entirely different interest

before there is room to do

know it will be easier now

"Ernest Villa"
Cawley Mill Rd
Uxbridge, Mdx,
Eng.
May 23rd, 1917

Dear Folks:

When I arrived here I found two or three letters awaiting me. One from Pa Pa. One from Ma Ma with clippings. I enjoyed reading them believe me. It seems good to know what news you folks are getting. I also got Ruthie & Louise's letters & thanks very much for same.

I fully appreciate Pa Pa's advice in answer to my special question. I realize it will be a hard fight to get a start in whatever work I decide upon. But whatever it may be, I am going to make good at it. I have a new & entirely different interest in life now, & if God sees fit to return me safely back home again, my Heart & soul will be in whatever work I feel guided into. It's impossible to decide until I return & have a thorough look round, & talk with you what work will appeal to me most. In one way I have learned & seen more these past two years than in all the other years of my life put together. But still in another sense they have been wasted. I don't know what you will think of their affect on me. I am sure. I think "France" opened my eyes & set me thinking more than anything else ever has. No one, no matter who they are, can imagine for one moment what it is really like until they have been thru it themselves. It seems to me absolute mockery of the Bible itself, yet we must believe it is his will. It makes Christianity seem merely a superstition. Occasionally, a man will die with a prayer on his lips. It is his last & only chance to evade what he is inwardly afraid of, death and the unknown. Before that he might probably have never said a prayer since his childhood. On the other hand a great many will die with a curse on their lips. Oh, it makes a fellow think I tell you & I have been thinking ever since· I can't tell you what I think of Eng· in general, or I would· We are certainly fighting for the right, but how the people in general can imagine that Eng· is a model, beats me·

The moral principles need a tremendous amount of improving before there is room to do much talking· Well, that is enough of that I guess·

How is everybody? I see Teddy R· is not getting what he was after· I am enclosing a clipping I thought might interest you· It amused me very much the way it looks at the Yankees·

I am having a fine time· The folks here can't do enough for me it seems· Mrs· R· treats me as she would her own Boy "Cyril"· My but she is nice· I know you would like her·

Cecile & I are going to London tomorrow· I want to see a little if possible while the weather is good·

I told you my recommend(?) for two weeks was cut to 8 days didn't I? But I am thankful to get any so I must not grumble·

I am sending a couple cards· I hope you get them· Did you receive my photos yet? I asked Helen to send them on to you·

I hear that the transferring to Yankees will not be permitted by the Can· Mil· Authorities so I guess that's all off·

Those mumps sure hit me hard & since then both my heart and lungs seem to bother considerable more than ever·

I am glad that Dr· Wickware thought fit to tell you what he did[21] I had several good talks with him·

---

[21] This is the doctor that had had written to Dr. Hazelton and had said that Walter was doing OK and that Walter was not shirking the duties of a soldier.

I have done my best to keep straight & often temptations were awfully hard to resist but the thought of the ones I love have carried me thru so far & I know it will be easier now & I earnestly ask for His help. Well, I must close for now. I hope this finds you all well & happy.

With Love to all. I am Always

Your Loving Son,
Walter
P.S. Cecile sends her kind regards to all of you.

Walter started off this letter with deep thoughts about his future. The idea about going into medicine like his father wasn't mentioned but rather the need to keep an open mind. He is confident he will succeed in whatever he sets his mind to.

He feels he has changed but can't put the life in the trenches behind him. It obviously affected him deeply and changed his perspective on life. He comments, " *I have learned & seen more these past two years than in all the other years of my life put together.* " and then goes on to say " *No one, no matter who they are, can imagine for one moment what it is really like until they have been thru it themselves.* " These are very mature thoughts from a 19-year-old. They will guide him the rest of his life.

During this period he has also been able to spend more time with Cecile and her mother and able to see how the locals conduct themselves. The moral principles are a bit of a shock to this boy who was raised with extremely high standards. The differences are so great that he doesn't want to talk to them about it. This will become a bigger and bigger issue as time goes by.

At this point he says he has been able to resist temptations so we can only wonder what this means. After all, his grandfather had said that he couldn't even put his arm around a girl until they were engaged and couldn't kiss her until they were married.

He also mentions that he knows that his parents would like Cecile's mother. The thought has already developed that they (Walter's parents) might get to meet her if he and Cecile were to get married and Cecile's parents were to come over. This will be further mentioned in a subsequent letter. And, his postscript at the end of the letter about Cecile writing to his parents also indicates that the relationship is getting more serious.

Again in this letter he mentions having continued health problems which have been a problem for a year and will continue for some time.

*****

His next letter is just three weeks later after he has been put into a recovery program.

(Billet) 150 London Road,
St. Leonards-On-Sea
Sussex.

June 16th 1917.

Dear Folks:

Tonight I was awfully glad to get Ma Ma's nice long letter & clippings sent May 28th. A couple days ago I received Pa Pa's & the girls letters. I am sure glad to have them coming once more. Pa Pa's was dated May 22nd & Ma Ma's was censured this time, the first for months now, but all was O.K. The Girls letters were fine, I guess Florence sent Helen's letter to me by mistake. ~~She~~ Gladys has certainly improved in her writing lately, she must be getting along fine at school. I am glad the sickness is over once more, & I hope it

(Billet) 150 London Road
St. Leonard's On-Sea
Sussex
June 16th, 1917

Dear Folks:

Tonight I was awfully glad to get Ma Ma's nice long letter & clippings sent May 28th. A couple days ago I received Pa Pa's & the girls letters. I am sure glad to have them coming once more. Pa Pa's was dated May 22nd & Ma Ma's was censured this time. The first for months but all was O.K. The Girls letters were fine. I guess Florence sent Helen's letter to me by mistake. Gladys[22] has certainly improved in her writing lately, she must be getting along fine at school. I am glad the sickness is over once more & I hope it stays away for awhile now.

Your prices are certainly up but it is worse here. I don't know exactly how they run but Potatoes are very hard to get & are only rationed out at a Gov. set prices, 3 1/2 c. a lb. Sugar is the same. You know we are only allowed to eat meat & Potatoes certain days. I am enclosing a clipping of today's paper.

Yes, I think I will have to stay with the Canadians now anyway. I am in full swing now working hard every day, but will not leave here until next month. My cough is getting better & I feel more myself again; it is doing me good. I may add that I am at present on 7 days No. 2 Field Punishment but we just have to report twice after parade. But that means $7.70 deferred till after the war. This is the way I got it. It was lights out and I had been reading. Four of the boys were playing cards in the corner. The game got exciting & two of us stood up to watch it. Then in walked the P.C. & we were all crimed & got 7 days. It rather

[22]His sister Galdys was just 12 years old at this time

galled me to take it as I was just going to bed & had nothing to do with the cards. But we have a pig-headed P.C. now & you can't explain anything. I will be glad to leave this place [even] if it does mean France.

I walked 12 miles yesterday with pack on a route march & then had an hour's fatigue at night. But my time is up Mon. night. I have been trying hard to get ahead & that is what comes of it. I may get better satisfaction at my reserve unit. I am going to try at any rate.

It certainly is too bad about little Laddie. Florence & Gladys told me in their letters. It must have been a hard blow to poor Leta.

Yes, I got the letter from Frank Wadsworth[23] *alright. I wish I could type as good, believe me.*

Was Uncle Willie's place hurt at all by the cyclone? I hope not.

So Winnie[24] *wasn't disturbed, you say. From what Helen said I thought she took it awfully bad, but it was evidently a lucky stroke. She evidently doesn't care to answer my letters & explanation. Yes, she was a nice girl but I am very glad it happened now. I half suspected she had some other friend, as her letters were so few and far between & they seemed to lack something, but I wish her every happiness & am very glad it was one of the Henley boys. They are nice boys. I must write to her once more now, but I think she will answer my last letter.*

I know you will like Cecile, all of you, she is a good girl & thinks as much of me as I do of her & that is a great deal. She is coming nineteen & is a healthy fine girl. I hope you will write to her.

---

[23]Frank Wadsworth is his aunt's husband who was a successful businessman in New York

[24]Winnie was Walter's girlfriend before he enlisted

Mrs. R. does not know I sent her letter on to you. I thought she might not really like it, but I wanted you to see it.

They expect to go to America after the war if nothing happens to Cyril[25] or Mr. R.... Cecile & I have fully made up our minds to wait for each other no matter how long it is. I mean to work as hard as possible to get a good start when I get back. Of course it will take years, but I am sure it will be well repaid in the end. I told you I meant to get a ring before I come back & I must get some money from some place. I want to get a pretty good one too, one that will last a long time. If I go to France again soon I will start saving but it is impossible to while in this country. The 3 (Lbs) a month[26] does not seem to go as far as $10 over there. I believe when a fellow goes on draft Leave he gets a LB a day, credit or no credit. If that is right I may manage alright, but I don't want to get a cheap ring & I don't want to go to France broke. I discovered once, that it was awfully inconvenient & hard on a fellow who did, so if you can spare some this time I won't ask again for a long time.

By the way, you asked what church R......'s were. They are Eng. Church but Cecile is broad-minded enough to change if she comes to that. She Believes as I believe, but I can't call myself a real Christian until I have joined a Church & really try hard to live up to my belief & that can hardly be while I am in the Army.

I have just had to double a mile, as the "fire piquet" just blew & I am on it tonight. We have had to "stand to" 3 times lately for "general alarms". Air Raids were supposed to be on. They are rather frequent lately.

---

[25]Cyril is Cecile's brother
[26]All but 3 lbs a month of his pay had been assigned to his father

Well I must quit now; it is nearly 10 P.M.

Say how about the photo of you all. Cecile is very anxious to see it, & she is having one taken especially to send to you.

I hope this finds you all well & happy again. With lots of love for all & best regards for those who inquire for me.

Always Your Trusting
& Hoping,
Walter

By this time Walter and Cecile were engaged. They had only known each other for eight or nine months but were deeply committed. Walter was spending as much time as possible at their house and was becoming part of the family. He and Cecile were already looking ahead to the end of the war and living in the U.S. They were also talking about her parents coming over. Cecile's mother had apparently written a letter to Walter subsequent to the engagement which must have been very favorable since he passed it on to his parents.

Walter had written to his girlfriend back home (Winnie) and told her about his engagement to Cecile. Apparently she had been seeing one of the local boys whom Walter knew and he was happy for her.

Walter goes on further in this letter to try to sell Cecile and her family to his parents since they were in a lower strata economically as well as religiously. Walter's parents had even asked about what church the R........'s belonged to. Walter is working hard in this, and subsequent letters, to minimize these differences to his parents and is sure that he and Cecile will be able to work things out.

He also mentions remaining in the Canadian army. With his parents now back in the U.S., where he was born, he had asked about transferring into U.S. forces but that didn't work out. He also mentions that there was still the possibility of his going back to France which had to worry him a lot.

*****

The next letter was another one written from Cecile's home so it seems that he has been able to visit there quite often:

"Ernest Villa"
Cowley Mill Road,
Uxbridge, Mdx.
Eng.
June 23rd.

Dear Mother & Father;

I am sorry I have not written to you this past while. I wrote to Dad, & was starting one to you when I was called away to take a Class in Anti-Gas training. I worked every minute nearly, when I was on the Course at Bexhill, & now I am on Leave. So you understand dont you!

I am having a good time here, at my English Home, I call it, & I certainly could not possibly be treated more like a son, than I am. Cecile had to go to work this A.M. but is coming home at one. We have had fine weather until today. Sat afternoon we spent a few hours in London but were glad to get out of the crowds & noise again. I enjoy my Leave just as much & more right here at home than as if we could see all of London. I am always happy when with Co.

them to say Good bye to their

"Ernest Villa"
Cawley Mill Road
Uxbridge, Mdx,
Eng
June 23rd

Dear Mother & Father:

I am sorry I have not written to you this past while. I wrote to Dad and was starting one to you when I was called away to take a Class in Anti-Gas training. I worked every minute dearly when I was on the Course in Bexhill, & now I am on leave. So you understand don't you?

I am having a good time here at my English Home. I call it & I certainly could not possibly be treated more like a son than I am. Cecile had to go to work this A.M. but is coming home at one. We have had fine weather until today. Sat. afternoon we spent a few hours in London but were glad to get out of the crowds & noise again. I enjoy my Leave just as much & more right here at home than if we could see all of London. I am always happy with aunt Cis & Mrs. R. is so good to me. Cyril is home for a few hours, but naturally spends most of his time with his fiancee. Mrs. R. was home last evening too & we all had a fine sing & Mrs. R. played a lot. She is an Expert on the Piano & Cecile is more than an Expert at singing. She has a lovely voice and knows how to use it believe me. She cannot play like her mother but is learning fast. She has not had the best of opportunities but has done well considering. When she did have them, like most of us, she did not realize their value but does now & is making the best of it.

Now, the folks here, were none of them brought up the same as we were at home, & are not so emphatic as regards to Religion. But they are good straight people, just the same, & although I wish it were different, it can't be helped. I love Cecile with all my heart and when we are together I can perhaps show her how important it is. I can do that when no one else can. It is not their fault. People always live as they have been taught to, to a great extent don't they? So rather it is their misfortune. That is one thing that I know her parents are a little afraid of. When she comes away over there with me they hardly expect to see her again but they want to be sure she will be happy & that you will all be friends with her and help her get used to it. You see, since Papa is a Dr. & Mrs. R. only a fancy painter or Artist in Civil Life they are afraid you will look down on Cis. But I try to make them see the difference in those things over there. I know you won't because she means so much to me & if she were the poorest Girl in Eng. I would love her still. I can't help myself if I wanted To. But I don't want to, so I see no reason why we should not be happy. It will be terribly hard for them to say Good bye to their only Girl. They think the world of her. I know & so do I. As you know, we are engaged, but we cannot think very seriously of being married until things are more settled and we are a little older. Her parents would not consent to that unless they saw we were really determined. So we must wait & get ready that is all.

I am going to Bexhill as Instructor in the N. C. O. School there soon. It may be for some time if I do not get into the R.A.F. I worked hard & made even better than 1st a "Distinguished". They picked me out & Rightly for that job, so I feel quite proud. It will mean promotions too, quite soon.

Well, I must meet Cecile's train now so Au Revoir for this time. Heaps of Love from

Your Loving & Trusting
Son
Walter

(Cecile sends her Love to all & will write soon)

Walter has been spending more time at his "English" home but continues to be concerned about their lower morals and religious beliefs. His comments about people living as they have been taught being a misfortune is very philosophical for a youngster. But he thinks he can change Cecile over time. Clearly this is a big concern as he continues to mention it in a number of his letters. He is trying hard to convince his parents that she will work out but is very worried about her acceptance back home.

Also, Walter mentions that they have discussed the timing of getting married and that they need to wait until things settle down and they get a little older. This means that they want to wait until after the war is over. Cecile's parents probably were concerned about a quick marriage since so many of the soldiers were not coming back home from the war including two of their own sons.

Walter has been working hard in his training which soon pays off as he is made an instructor at one of the training schools. This will include more pay which he desperately needs to cover his costs while on leave visiting Cecile.

Walter and Cecile

Chapter Seven
R. A. F. Training

Quite a bit of time elapses between the previous letter and the next one. He apparently was writing home almost weekly but many of the letters were passed around the family so his mother wasn't able to save them all.

Nevertheless, this next letter confirms that he has not been sent back to France. Clearly more troops were continually needed as the battles continued. His B.E.F. unit was still facing the Germans in the same area and the history books talk about the third battle of Ypres in the second half of 1917. There were a lot of casualties so replacements would have been important. But, Walter's health problems continued to be serious enough to keep him out of the front. However, he was well enough to be training new troops. The fact that he had been in the trenches and experienced firsthand what the fighting was like certainly was helpful in the training process.

During this time he had also applied to the R.A.F. and was beginning the process of being accepted as we see in this next letter:

No 2 Company,
18th Canadian Reserve Battalion
Dibgate Camp Shorncliffe Kent
~~c/o Army Post Office,~~
~~London~~, Eng.

Mar. 17 1918

Dear Folks:

It is sometime now since I had heard from any of you. But I had a letter from Ruthie a couple of days ago. So she has gone into the College to stay. Why is Auntie leaving Denver?

I guess Helen is back home again by this time is she not? Has Mama fully recovered from her operation yet? I hope she feels better for having it. How is Business?

I have been laid up for a couple of days with Influenza but I am alright now. They wanted me to go to hospital but I didn't, as I knew it would probably delay my R.F.C. Com. longer. I am next on the list to see the Air Board in London. But that does not amount to much. They usually give the med. Exam. after the Course. Several have already gone for their Officers Training Course from here, so

I had a ... ago. Things seem pretty

No 2 Company
18th Canadian Reserve Battalion
Dibgate Camp, Shorncliffe, KenT
Mar· 17, 1918

Dear Folks:

It is sometime now since I had heard from any of you· But I had a letter from Ruthie a couple of days ago· So she has gone into College to stay· Why is Auntie leaving Denver?

I guess Helen is back home again by this time, is she not? Has Ma Ma fully recovered from her operation yet? I guess she is better for having it· How is business?

I have been laid up for a couple of days with influenza but I am alright now· They wanted me to go to hospital but I didn't as I knew it would probably delay my R·F·C[27] Com· longer· I am next on the list to see the Air Board in London· But that does not amount to much· They usually give the Med· Exam after the Course· Several have already gone for their Officers Training Course from here, so if everything goes alright I ought to be away pretty soon· Did you receive the letter saying how to send the money? I will probably need it before it gets here but will have to make out the best I can until it arrives· It ought not to take very long after you see the Bank· I hope it is not going to bother you much to send that money· I know how badly you need it but what can I do? That is all I have to get started on· My Assigned Pay must come to over 300 now since it started so I must have helped a little· It will soon be two years since we first hit Eng· & believe I have experienced more in that time than all the rest of my life· I knew nothing of the world before I left but I know too much now, I think, or at least I mean I would be quite willing to settle

---

[27]Request For Commission?

down at home and stay there· But it is liable to be some time yet before I can do that·

We are having pretty nice weather just now for this time of year· I hope it lasts·

I am hoping to get up to see Cecile one of these days but prospects don't look any to cheerful· Leave is very hard to get just now· Things are pretty monotonous around here· We are pretty busy training new men from Canada though, so it fills the time·

How are the girls getting along at school? As much as ever? They will need to help Ma Ma a lot now that Helen is gone·

Have you heard from Cisie lately? I know she meant to write· I had a very nice letter from her father a couple days ago·

Did I tell you that I received that pen knife alright after all? It is splendid, thanks ever so much· And the gloves are fine and warm· The boys often ask me where they came from·

I had a letter from Mrs· Hamblin not long ago· Things seem pretty dead around there·

I also heard from C· Arnas· He is not in France yet, but expects to be soon·

Well, I must close for this time· Have you been receiving all of my letters? I write about once a week you know·

Hoping this finds you all well & happy· I am always

your Loving Son

Walter

P·S· I received a very nice letter from Mrs· Moore of Edgeley· I really don't know her but I acknowledged a parcel she sent at Xmas·

At this point Walter is just twenty years old. He has been away from home and his family for quite a while and clearly misses everyone. He continues to seek news about what is going on back there. His parents had moved back to the U.S., one of his sisters has been married for a year and another has left for college. He is trying to stay in touch with his letters and certainly relishes any letters he gets in return.

At the same time he has not been able to get away from camp very much to see Cecile. The historic old camp at Shorncliffe, where he was stationed at this time, was nearly 200 kilometers from Uxbridge where Cecile's family lived. However, the relationship seemed to have stayed strong. Even Cecile's father had written a nice letter to him.

Once again in this letter Walter mentions having had the flu. Clearly his health was continuing to be a problem which is probably why he hadn't been sent back to France by now. But he didn't want to go back to the hospital as the doctors suggested. He was hoping for a promotion and didn't want that to interfere.

Walter was also moving forward on his quest to join the R.A.F. Some of the other guys from that camp had already been chosen and had gone for the Officers Training Course so he seemed optimistic that this was within reach.

He was also needing more money from home. Every time he had some leave or was able to get away from the camp to go into town he would need money to pay for food, or movies, or presents for Cecile and family, etc. A portion of his pay was "assigned" in care of his parents but he was not getting enough himself. He has told his parents how to send money and is wondering when it might arrive. He says he hopes it will not be too much of a bother "*knowing how much you need it.*" It sounds like money is also tight back home. Then he says "*that is all I have to get started*" so hopefully some of what is being sent home is building up a nest egg for when he returns. He also says "*I must have helped a little.*"

This suggests that at least some of his assigned pay was available for his parents to use. This question will never be answered completely but the need for money from home will recur and get even worse when he actually starts the R.A.F. training.

In this letter he again comments on his eye-opening experiences since he left home. His statement " *believe I have experienced more in that time than all the rest of my life. I knew nothing of the world before I left but I know too much now,"* is certainly profound. He is looking forward to a simple life back home whatever it might entail. However, going into the medical field seems not to be a priority anymore.

The troops certainly appreciated getting items from home. Even some of the most basic items were generally not available. The pen knife had finally come as well as some gloves. These were very welcome and some of the other boys were envious. Some of the Canadian folks in a nearby town back home were also sending packages to the troops so that they would know that they weren't forgotten.

*****

Three months later Walter writes a letter while at Seaford[28] having just passed the Anti-Gas course with flying colors. He is feeling pretty optimistic about getting into the R.A.F. but has been offered a different opportunity because of his good work:

---

[28]Seaford is one the southern coast about 60 kilometers south of London and a bit farther from Cecile's home in Uxbridge.

Seaford, June 16th - 1918.

Dear Folks:

Last week I received both Mama's & Papa's nice long letters, & also those of the girls. I certainly was glad to get them. I would have answered it immediately but I guess you heard from Lis, or got my card, stating I was at Bexhill on an advanced Anti-Gas Instructors Course.

You see I was told it would be the 25th of this month before I would see the air Board, so as I had the chance to go the Bexhill, I did, & believe me I am glad. I made either a high "First Class" or a Distinguished. I worked hard & got what I was after, "Qualification". The morning I left, the two Officers in Command of the Gas Wing called me out, and asked me if I would like to be taken on the Instructional Staff of the Canadian Trench Warfare School, there at Bexhill. Well believe me I said I would

Seaford, Sussex
June 16th, 1918

Dear Folks:

Last week I received both Ma Ma's & Papa's nice long letters & also those of the girls. I certainly was glad to get them. I would have answered it immediately but I guess you heard from Cis, or got my card stating I was at Bexhill on my advanced Anti-Gas Instructor's course.

You see I was told it would be the 25th of this month before I would see the Air Board, so as I had the chance to do the Bexhill, I did, & believe me I am glad. I made either a high "First Class" or a Distinguished. I worked hard and got what I was after: "Qualification". The morning I left, the two Officers in Command of the Gas Wing called me out and asked me if I would like to be taken on the Instructional Staff of the Canadian French Warfare School there at Bexhill. Well, believe me I said I would and told him about my Commission[29] Well he said he didn't think I had the slightest chance of getting in as I came from France with Heart trouble. At any rate he said he would do his best to get me there at Bexhill. If he does, it means a good job for an indefinite period as well as temporary promotion & more pay. It would be a fine job & would be a good chance but I hate to cancel the Com. since I have been at it for so long. I think I will see the M.O.[30] tomorrow & explain things and ask him to see if there is any trace of trouble in my Heart or Lungs. If there is I might as well cancel it for I will certainly be turned down. Only about 1/4 of them get thr now. In that case I can take this job as long as she lasts. Perhaps I have hoped for too much all along but it is hard to give in. However I will know one way or the other before the end of this month. I expect six days of leave this week, so if

[29]The "Commission" was his request to join the R.A.F.
[30]Medical Officer

I get it I will spend a few days with Cis once more. I am awfully anxious to see her again. We are waiting for your answer to my other letter. I am awfully glad you think so much of her already. She will not disappoint you I am sure. She may not have an awfully good education & all that. But that would make no difference to me. I would think just as much of her one way as the other. I myself have not much education anyway, but I know I can make good & we will be quite happy anyway. It is a case of "make the most of what we can as we go." We both consider our engagement as you said "In the sight of God you are one forever." Well, that is why we were engaged and when the opportunity comes we will be married. I fully realize that we are young yet but as it has happened now instead of later, those two or three years cannot be jumped & we may just as well be together as not. There will be a struggle to get started after the war, but I am confident of winning, & she wants to help me so I see no other open road. If I came over alone to get ready, it would mean a trip back again & that would mean a big amount of money. With a little help from you we will be alright.

I am awfully glad you have that farm on the string & sincerely hope you have it, if not for yourself, for me. I will see that I pay for it afterwards. That is the start I wish & certainly appreciate your doing it for me.

I am certainly glad to hear you think you can get along so well there in Exeland.[31] It will be fine to be so near home when we do come over.

Now I said I wanted to go back and do my share in France but if my heart will not let me into the R.A.F. I know about how long I would last in the Infantry. It would mean hospital again as soon

[31]Dr. Hazelton had moved to Exeland and resumed his medical practice because the farming in Canada was not working out.

as wet weather set in. Well, when you look at it square in the face, I would certainly be helping more as an Instructor than in Hospital. I feel fine now, never felt better in fact. But I cannot help but see that going to France is not the only way one can help. There are thousands of new men who must be trained & I guess I might as well help do it since I can do so. I feel awfully proud since I have been asked if I wanted a job on the Staff at Bexhill for you see it is the Central Canadian Anti-Gas Instructor's school & their object is to standardize the training. There are not many Instructors there and that is why I feel so big, because I have had the opportunity of being one of them. A Pal of mine from the old 68th went down a few weeks ago.

Withstanding all this, I would [like] to get into the flying Corps most of all. I know what that is too.

Oh, yes there are a few killed in training over here too but then you cannot expect anything else when there are so many thousand young English Boys in it. They want them more than anyone, that is why so many of us are turned down. There is a phrase in their orders stating all Applicants must be of British born parents. I don't really think that would hold me out, but it has done to some.

The Germans will get all they want pretty soon now. We know the Americans are coming.[32] If they hold them up on this drive the great danger will probably be over.

I sincerely hope Jack will get along good this year. He certainly means to at any rate.

Glad to hear the Dodge is so good. Is it a one or two seater? I would give a pile to be in it now. Ha. Ha.

---

[32]The American troops were just arriving at the battle fronts.

I had a nice letter from Helen too the other day. It is too bad they lost the old saw.

I hope Ruthie makes good in Denver. I received a nice letter from her.

I will write to Ma Ma in a few days but it is quitting time now. With love to all, trusting this finds all well & happy.

Always

Your Loving Son

P.S. Do you want me to have your address changed at Headquarters London. You can change it in Ottawa.

The picture is getting more rosy for Walter after he did so well at the Anti-Gas school in Bexhill.[33] The officers there were certainly impressed and offered him a job as an instructor. That was very welcome at this point since it would be a good job with an increase in pay and he could be an instructor for quite a while. However, he told the officer he wanted to continue to pursue the Commission in the R.A.F. It is interesting at this point that this officer told him he didn't have the slightest chance, having come from France with heart trouble. Anyway, Walter figured he should go see the Medical Officer to confirm if there were still any problems with his heart or lungs and if so, give up on the R.A.F. idea.

He is looking forward to his leave so he may see Cecile. Because of the distances between the bases and Cecile's home, he hasn't been able to see her for some time. These big gaps had to be hard on both of them but they seemed to be handling it just fine. He is still working on "selling" Cecile to his parents and is apparently

[33]Bexhill was about 55 kilometers southeast of London so still some distance from Cecile.

succeeding to some extent. Walter has some concerns about getting started back home but seems confident that they can work it out. He is even thinking about farming as a possibility since his father still owns a farm in Canada.

Walter also comments that, while he had previously said that he wanted to go back to France to do his share, if he did end up back in the trenches he wouldn't last long once the wet weather set in. He felt he would be able to contribute more as an instructor than being in a hospital again.

His comments, while brief, about how many are killed in the training for the R.A.F., doesn't seem to scare him. The terrible life in the trenches is etched in his mind. A little bigger concern seems to be getting accepted into the R.A.F. by the authorities since the preference is for English boys. So, between his health issues and the low probability of getting in at this point, it is amazing that he continued to pursue it. Even more amazing is that he finally was accepted as we will see from his letters to follow.

*****

Just a month later he is writing from an R.A.F. location where he is now a cadet. Amazingly he has passed all the physical exams and can now pursue becoming a pilot in the R.A.F. This initial training will take about six months but it also means he will not be sent back to France to fight in the trenches.

Present Address ÷ Cadet Haylton W.A.
"B" Flight #104312.
No 4 Squadron.
No 1, O.T.T.W.
R.A.F.
119 Marina.
Hastings
Sussex.

P.S.
You had better continue Addressing c/o Cecile.

July 14th.

Dear Folks:

Well I am down here in the old church Club that I used to write so often from a year ago. It was a Soldiers Club then but is an Officer's Cadet club now.

You will see the difference in my Address too. But that I will only be for about three weeks.

As I said in the lettercard a few days ago I passed the Medical Air Board, physically fit as a Pilot, and hold a certificate showing it. My eyes & ears are perfect. The med. Exam was rather hard but a trifle hurried owing to the large number to be put thru.

First, at an Elementary Board my eyes, ears, heart, lungs, & nerves, were tested. That was

Present address: Cadet Hazelton, W. A. #104312
"B Flight", No 4 Squadron
No. 1 OT.T.W. R.A.F.
119 Marina
Hastings, Sussex
July 14

Dear Folks:

Well, I am down here in the old church club that I used to write so often from a year ago. It was a Soldier's Club then but is an Officer's Cadet club now.

You will see the difference in my address too. But that will only be for about three weeks.

As I said in the letter card a few days ago, I passed the Medical Air Board physically fit as a Pilot and hold a certificate showing it. My eyes & ears are perfect. The Med. Exam was rather hard but a trifle hurried owing to the large number to be put thru

First, at an Elementary Board, my eyes, ears, heart, lungs & nerves, were tested. That was OK. I passed easily. Then finally, lungs were tested by sounding & by holding the breath more than one minute. I held mine 100 secs. He felt my pulse after & during all sorts of exertion & also listened to it. I was a little afraid something was wrong but no. Then nerves & balance were tested by standing solely on one leg with arms stretched forward & fingers spread hanging limp with eyes closed for about half a minute. Another Balancing stunt was given too. Then, yes, ears, nose, throat & teeth were examined again. Well, I was quite surprised when I passed as a Pilot. I rather thought it would be as an observer.

We were sent here yesterday to the Officer's technical training Wing where we remain a few weeks before proceeding with Morse signaling & topography. After about 8 weeks of that, if we pass *all further exams & tests, we go to Oxford to Study Aeronautics & after that to learn flying. So you see I am going to have a handful of work but I mean to make good if it is possible.*

I find out now that Cis & her folks do not like me in the Flying Corps at all. I wish they had said so first. Someone has been telling them some things which make it seem pretty dangerous but if they realized just the difference between that & the trenches it would not be so bad. A War is a dangerous thing for all concerned it seems to me so why not make the best out of it As I said before, the course of training a man gets would alone compensate all expense[34] *& work expended for it will be very useful. A fellow realizes better the value of an education when you get here. Well, I have tried for a long time & I mean to see it thru now.*

I hope you have been able to send the money I asked for without running things too short. My assigned Pay will probably stop next month, then they pay us our full pay so it will be alright. Equipment & things to work with cost us considerably lately but with what you can send I will manage O.K. In case you have not received that card of mine, have a bank there cable it to a bank here: Lloyd's Bank, St. Leonards-On-Sea or Hastings Branch. It will not cost a great deal & I will need some badly before you could mail it to me. I will ask the Bank to advise me as soon as it comes, so no full Address is necessary. Just W.A. Hazelton #104312.

I spent several evenings at Ernest Villa last week while I was at Hampstead, London. Cecile has had the Influenza pretty badly so pardon her if she has not written lately, won't you?

I must write to Ruthie & Helen soon too. I have been on the go since about six weeks ago pretty steadily & have not had the time to write that I used to have. We will be studying pretty hard

---

[34]As a cadet there were a number of expenses that he had to pay for himself.

after a week or two for three or four months until we get our Commissions. Several Canadians are here. A lot in fact.

Well, I certainly don't expect the War to end this year now. The Americans are coming fast tho & are helping a great deal. I have spoken to several who were taking M. Gun Courses at Uxbridge Royal Air Force school.

It is raining today & we are in tents for a couple weeks. The Canadians get thru quicker than the Imperial boys & those who are just joining up, or rather being called up.

Well, I must ring off for this time.

Hoping you are all well & happy, I am always,

Your Loving & trusting Son,
Walter

P.S. I am feeling fine excepting a little cold.

[A note at the bottom was inserted by Walter's father]
(Send this to Helen)
(Helen, return to us)
Show to uncle, Pa Pa

The physical exams that Walter had to get through were obviously very tough but he passed all of them. Even the lungs, which had been a chronic problem, were OK. The heart issues had also subsided, much to his surprise, as well as to his past commander. The physical exams had to be tough because they didn't want to spend a lot of time training these cadets only to have some health problem interfere with their capability to actually fly.

He mentions that Cis and her folks weren't happy about him going into the R.A.F. and he was sorry they didn't mention it earlier. They probably didn't expect him to make it so didn't say anything. Clearly they had been seeing the news and hearing about all the training accidents for the airmen let alone the actual combat fatalities.[35] However, he felt the brutal conditions in the trenches had to be worse than the risks of flying.

Once again the question of needing money from home is mentioned. The cadets had to buy some of their equipment as well as some of their uniforms so he was needing even more money than just what he was spending while visiting Cecile. Fortunately the portion of his pay that was "Assigned" to his parents was about to stop so he would be getting all of it now. Even then it was still only privates' pay[36].

Another interesting note is the one about the Canadians getting through the training quicker than Imperial boys.

*****

And then there is the long awaited one from Cecile to Walter's father:

---

[35]The average life span of new pilots at this time was only two weeks.

[36]The typical amount of a private's pay in U.S. forces at this time was only about $15.00 a month and probably even less for the English servicemen.

"Ernest Villa"
Cowley Mill Road
Uxbridge
Middx
July 25th 1918.

Dear Mrs Hazelton,

Very many thanks for the magazine. I quite enjoyed it, & it came in very nicely too, I was ill in bed with the flu at the time & I had no new books to read, and when Mum brought your book up to me I was quite pleased. I knew I should find a lot of nice things inside, some of the stories are quite good, & I also like the "Ladies Home Journal", I should miss that now, there are some tales which continue each month & you would not believe how I look for that book. I like reading very much, & the American writers seem to explain themselves so clearly, which makes one become interested at once in the tale.

"Ernest Villa"
Cawley Mill Road
Uxbridge
Mdx
July 25th, 1918

Dear Mr. Hazelton,

Very many thanks for the magazine. I quite enjoyed it, & it came in very nicely too. I was ill in bed with the flu at the time & I had no other books to read, and when Mum brought your book up to me I was quite pleased. I knew I should find a lot of nice things inside. Some of the stories inside are quite good & I also like the "Ladies Home Journal". I should miss that now, there are some stories which continue each month & you would not believe how I look for that book. I like reading very much, and the American writers seem to explain themselves so clearly, which makes one like me interested in it once in the tale. I imagine you have heard about the epidemic of flu going all over England, hundreds of folks have died with it too. I had it very badly. I had to go to bed & stay there for more than a week. one has terrible pains in the head when it is coming on & when one gets better one feels very weak. I was so pleased Walter would get down to see me while I was sick. It happened that he was only a few miles away so you see he could get down to see me, but I am quite recovered now and back to business as usual.

How are you getting on in your new town, Mr. Hazelton? I do hope you have lots & lots of good luck & get on famously. You deserve it alright & I think you will. Are you keeping in good health?

I guess Walter has written & told you that he is training for officer in the "Royal Air Force". There is not any R.X.s now, you know. The "Royal Naval Air Service" & the "Flying Corps" have been united; therefore they have a new name: The R.A.X which

Walter belongs to now & I hope it is for the best, but one sees so many accidents with the planes that it makes one wonder if he would have been better out of it, but I guess he will have to go through with it now.

It is getting quite late now so I will say good night & God bless you & sincerely hoping Mrs. & children are well. My Mother sends her kind regards to you all.

Yours affectionately,

Cecile

This letter from Cecile to Dr. Hazelton took months for her to get up the courage to write. After all, she was just an ordinary girl from rural England, writing to a doctor in the U.S. where everybody was thought to be rich and successful. So Cecile finally writes with the content being very courteous.

She apologizes for not writing sooner because of having the flu. As she points out there was a serious epidemic going on in England. Many had died from it. Food was scarce so the overall health of the people was not that good. Things like meat, butter and sugar were very hard to get if at all.

Cecile also mentions her concern about Walter going into the R.A.F. but that he would go on with it anyway.

****

About two months go by before another letter is written by Walter to his parents. He has been very busy with the training which is still only bookwork. Since the training is being done at a number of locations he tells his parents to send any letters to Cecile's address:

Always Address c/o Coutts unless I say otherwise
No. 1 R.A.F. Cadet Wing,
Hastings
Sept. 23rd 1918.

Dear Folks:

I have had no word from you since I have been with the Air Force. I wonder what is the matter. I have been anxiously awaiting notice from ~~Lloy~~ Lloyd's Bank stating that they have received the money I cabled for. But no it has not arrived yet and I am badly in need of it. I have had to borrow some from my pals. Did you cable it or send it by post? It should be here, even by mail now. I hope I did not ask too much but I understood you could send some when I needed it. It is only while I am on this Officer's training Course that I will need so much, and then I will make the Pay do. Of course when we have our Commission the Pay is sufficient & more, but it costs quite a bit to get the Com. from what I can see. A "Pound" seems to go about as far as two "Dollars" used to. But don't for a moment think I am getting extravagant, for really I spend just what I need too and very seldom spend much on pleasure. As I said before I have learned and have got

and in between it would bring it modern

Always Address c/o Cecile unless I say otherwise

Sept. 23rd, 1918

Dear Folks:

I have had no word from you since I have been with the Air Force. I wonder what is the matter? I have been anxiously awaiting notice from Lloyd's Bank stating that they have received the money I cabled for. But no, it has not arrived yet and I am badly in need of it. I have had to borrow some from my pals. Did you cable it or send it by post? It should be here even by mail now. I hope I did not ask too much but I understood you could send some when I needed it. It is only while I am on this Officers Training Course that I will need so much and then I will make the Pay do. Of course when we have our Commission the Pay is sufficient & more, but it costs quite a bit to get the Com. from what I can see. A pound seems to go about as far as two Dollars used to. But don't for a moment think I am getting extravagant, for really I spend just what I need too and very seldom spend much on pleasure. As I said before, I have learned and have got to learn more to qualify as a Pilot than I have ever learned before, and all in a very few months. It is wonderful the amount they teach such a large number in such a short time. The Air Force is rapidly becoming THE force, and I am proud to think I am going to be an Active part of it. I fully expect to be flying at the Front by Spring. Of course I will have to do a lot of Practice flying this winter.

I have my new Uniform now, but will not start wearing it for a few weeks. I will have a Photo taken as soon as I can. Naturally I feel rather proud of it & hope you will see a great improvement since the last one.

The Yankees are sure doing fine now, & there seems to be a faint Glimmer of peace next year.[37] *I hope so at any rate. Everything seems to be going fine now.*

I have been unable to see Cecile since the second week of July but am hoping for at least a weekend soon.

Well, I am having an easy time for a few days now. The Wing has moved again and a few of us were left behind to occupy the billets until taken over by the new party. Consequently we are doing practically nothing. But our final Exams are next week so there is some plugging ahead. After that the work begins. This is merely a preliminary course to get us into the habit of studying again.

Well, how is everything going? How is business? I have not heard from Helen or Ruth for some time either. I have not written to anyone else for a long time, just to Cis & you folks. I don't know what all my friends will think of me, but I cannot write much & do this studying for there is not time.

We are having the Equinoctual Storms just now. It is very changeable. It rains one moment and is fine the next.

I saw a fine Moving picture a few nights ago, in fact it so interested me that I saw it twice. It was called "Intolerance" & is very similar to the "Birth of Nations" I believe. It goes back and shows Babalonic wars, Balshazzar and a great deal of that. It also shows Christ & the Pharisees, Nazareth and lots more of that time. Again it brought in the Massacre of St. Bartholomew and in between it would bring in modern times. The object was to show what Intolerance had caused through the ages, and also to compare the modern hypocrites with the ones of Christ's time. It was certainly fine. The scenery was wonderful & where it showed Babylon, and the fall of Babylon to Cyrus was fine. Everything was

---

[37]U.S. troops had gotten into the front lines in May of 1918

just as History writes & illustrates it. Of course, there were certain Characters all the way through which made it more interesting. A great many could not grasp the meaning at all, but it is supposed to be the Greatest Film in the World. Of course, it is an American film. I believe parts of the Passion Play were brought into it. If you ever have the opportunity see it by all means, it is well worth it.

Well, I must close for now. I will write again as soon as I hear from you. Hoping that will be soon and that this finds you all well as it leaves me.

I am always

Your Loving & Trusting Son.

Walter

P.S. Cecile sends her love to all. I hope you can read this, I am writing it on my knee.

The mail was not getting through very well nor was the money that he seemed to need so badly. There were a lot of expenses during the training program and he was still on private's pay. He even had to buy his new uniform but he expected that as soon as the cadets received their commission and the corresponding pay raise that would come with it, that he would finally be OK with his expenses.

As to the war effort, he now thinks it might not be over until sometime in 1919. His training will involve some practice flying during the winter and then actual combat in the spring. The troops had no idea, at this point, that an armistice would be signed in less than two months.

In this letter Walter writes at length about a movie he saw called "Intolerance." He shows a good understanding of religious history in describing the movie and what the meaning of it was. Certainly his childhood in a "godly" household had something to do with it.

The training is keeping Walter so busy that he hasn't seen Cecile in over two months and has instead been writing to her.

*****

Two weeks later the R.A.F. training has progressed and he is now at Exeter College:

Oct. 6th 1918.

(No 2 School of Aeronautics
Royal Air Force)
Exeter College.
Oxford.

Dear Father:

Well as you see by my address I have passed the first part of my training, and am now at the old English town of Oxford. the school we are in is part of the great University and they carry on much in the same manner as a College would. Of course the Discipline is up to the mark. It is certainly the worst I have ever seen, but it all does us good. We have just arrived here, and are starting the hardest 6 weeks of studying that I have ever experienced, from what I am told. The work will be interesting however, and that counts a lot. Aerial Navigation, Engines, etc.

in you, and I mean to.

Oct. 6th, 1918
(No 2 School of Aeronautics,
Royal Air Force)
Exeter College
Oxford

Dear Father:

Well, as you can see by my address I have passed the first part of my training and am now at the old English town of Oxford. The school we are in is part of the great University and they carry on much in the same manner as a College would. Of course the Discipline is up to the mark. It is certainly the worst I have ever seen but it all does us good. We have just arrived here and are starting the hardest 6 weeks of studying that I have ever experienced from what I am told. The work will be interesting, however, and that counts a lot. Aerial Navigation, Engines, etc.

A few days ago I received a telegraph money order from you thru Wadsworth[38], New York. It amounted to 19 lbs 5s 11d. I was certainly relieved to get it and was wondering what to do. Thanks so much. I will be alright now indefinitely unless something unexpected turns up. Which one of the Wadsworths sent it for you? What address did you put on it? I have not received the five pounds you spoke of sending in Aug yet. Exactly what address did you put on that? It may find me any day now. Did you send any in care of Cecile as you spoke of doing?

Oh yes, I did manage to get a few hours leave last weekend and had a good time at Uxbridge. I may possibly go to Uxbridge for a month to the school of Gunnery which of course we must pass out of before flying. If so I will see Cecile quite a lot and will undoubtedly spend Xmas there.

---

[38]Wadsworth's were the family of his mother's sister's marriage.

I will have a photo taken before long in my new uniform which we start wearing here. You will hardly know me, I don't suppose. Of course, I feel quite dressed up and proud in them. But that will soon wear off. At any rate it seems so nice to have some good soft clothes on once more after all this time in General service stuff.

This is a very beautiful place, believe me. There are some thirty-two colleges in town & all are fine old English Buildings. A fellow feels considerable satisfaction being in them, the place where all the great students came. But we will be so busy that we will see practically none of the rest of the town. It is a case of work for all that you have in you and I mean to. It is worth it, believe me. I was picked out as a Flight Commander this morning so that means more work but it counts in the long run. I have twenty Canadian Cadets under me so will be O.K.

Things seem to be going fine over in France just now & I hope it continues. I expect to be there when it finishes up.

Well, I must wind up for this time & will write again before long. You understand why it is so short, I know.

How is everything and how is Practice. Tell Ruthie I will write before long. Hoping you are all well and happy. I am always

Your Loving Son, Walter

Walter is taking the training very seriously and is doing well. The subjects are mostly technical and therefore require a good mind for details, which Walter seems to have. His experience on the farm with machinery was certainly helpful. Evidently he has impressed those in charge since he was picked as a flight commander with a number of cadets under him.

The courses at this time were conducted at a famous old school and he marveled at the fine old buildings and the town itself, even though he didn't have much free time to take it all in. He has done very well with the training and seems to enjoy it despite the strict discipline that these young cadets are subjected to. Now that they are training to become officers they are expected to meet a higher standard of conduct and in their appearance. Their new uniforms were much nicer but they had to purchase parts themselves even though they were still on Private's pay. Fortunately, he recently received more money from home so is able to make do. It is surprising that these cadets had to pay for so many things.

He has only been able to get a few hours leave because of the intensity of the courses so has only been able to visit Cecile briefly during the past few months which had to add to the strain of the intense training. But after the upcoming six weeks of training, the training will be in Uxbridge, very near to Cecile, and he is certainly looking forward to that. It will include the Christmas holiday which will add to the enjoyment. However Christmases were pretty solemn in England by now since this would be the third one since the war started and many young boys would not be returning. There still didn't seem to be an end in sight for the war. He is even envisioning a lot of practice flying during the winter and would be battling over the front lines in the spring.

****

The next letter is just two weeks later:

No 2 School of Military
Aeronautics.
R.A.F.
Exeter College, Oxford,
England.
Oct. 21st. 1918.

Dear Folks:

I received Mother's letter a few days ago and another from Ruthie. I am going to do as suggested, write letters of general interest once a week, and they can be sent on to the others, for it is impossible to write many letters now, I am so busy. I know you will all be willing.

How is everyone now?

How is practise?

What do you think about the War now? It ought to be over before long now.

Well I am on my third week here, and talk about study, well that is

No. 2 School of Military
Aeronautics, R.A.F.
Exeter College, Oxford,
England
Oct. 21st, 1918

Dear Folks:

I received Mother's letter a few days ago and another from Ruthie. I am going to do as suggested, write letters of general interest once a week and they can be sent on to the others, for it is impossible to write many letters now, I am so busy. I know you will all be willing.

How is everyone now?

How is practice?

What do you think about the war now? It ought to be over before long now. Well, I am on my third week here and talk about study, well, that is no name for it. But compulsory sports are brought in every afternoon which keeps a fellow in shape. Lectures are on various subjects and practical work around aeroplanes from 8:30 A.M. until 1 P.M. lunch, then sports, compulsory study from 5:30 until 7:15, then dinner and more study after that until lights out at 10:15. But it only lasts six weeks here in Oxford. There is so much to learn in Aerial Navigation, construction & rigging of Planes, Engines, compasses, Altimeters and dozens of other little things let alone signaling, map reading, photography, etc. so perhaps you can imagine how busy a fellow is. Studying, sketching, drawing diagrams, copying notes, and signaling (wireless) keeps our time absolutely full and more. But I think this course is the best step I could have taken, it will be invaluable after the war and the experience during the war will be worth a lot. I am completely taken up with it and am going to make good or know why. My slight knowledge of engines helps a little and I am getting along OK so far. I told you I take a months' course at Uxbridge did I *not. That will finish about Xmas so I am quite certain of being at Ernest Villa for Xmas, all going well. After that a few weeks in a flying Squadron and then the Commission. I ought to be flying in France by Spring, all going well. Equipment of one kind or another takes lots of money because everything has gone up so. But I will get along alright now for quite awhile.*

Say, can Papa tell me exactly what he has sent to me since I came into the R.A.F? My pay will be increased as soon as I finish at Uxbridge and am a "Flight Cadet" it will be about $2.75 a day then. When Commissioned, it will be somewhere about $5.75 a day. Well, all meals, etc. must be in First Class Places, you see, and railway fare 1st in fact you have to pay out every turn. But I will undoubtedly be able to save some.

Flu is still Prominent here but lots of fresh air in all lecture rooms helps a lot, but gives plenty of colds too.

I told you some time ago that I had received the $92.00 from New York did I not? I am awfully glad Cousin Arthur looked at it in that light for I would never have got along without it. I hate to think of you having to give a note for it but I am sure it will be well repaid before long. This Course has started me into a Line I can put all my interest in. There will be plenty of chances for a fellow with Aerial Knowledge after the War.

I hope cousin Arthur writes to me. I will certainly write as good a letter in return as it is possible. I appreciate his interest in me.

I did not receive the $25.00 at all. I believe Papa had better ask them to trace it. It may turn up but if it does, alright.

I am glad Ruthie likes her work. I hope she gets along alright at Nursing. I do hope the crops in Sask. are O.K. Helen and Jack will be seeing daylight again if they are.

How is the Car? I wish I could attend to it. You see in learning Aerial Engines it brings in all about Auto Engines. I am getting it all here.

Well, in a few days I will be 21 and am glad to be able to spend it in the Wonderful Old Oxford University. It is a wonderful town. The most beautiful place I have seen. Along the Thames there are beautiful walks. I went thru part of the Museum on Sunday with an old 6th Sgt. who is taking a Commission in the Imperials. It was fine. I wish you could see it. But we have such little time for those things now.

AuRevoir Everybody. Hope you are all well & happy.

Heaps of Love from

Your Ever Loving

Walter

P.S. Please remember me to all of my friends you write to.

Clearly Walter is enjoying the training, even though it is very difficult with long hours of study. For people without any experience with flying it would seem like it should be quite easy to become a pilot given the simplicity of planes in those days? But the cadets were having to understand a lot more than just how to fly an airplane. The training was to take many weeks before they would even start to actually get in a plane and learn how to fly it. The good news is that they were in a wonderful old town and school where they could take a look around whenever they got a little free time.

Walter is beginning to think that there might be a career for him after war in aviation. The idea of farming seems to have been sidelined.

And, once again the concern about money comes up. These cadets were expected to behave like officers. When they went out into the town they even had to eat in first class places which, of course, were more expensive.

Walter in his cadet uniform

Exeter College where Walter ate his meals while training for the R.A.F.

COPY. F.S. Form 192. (a)

ROYAL AIR FORCE.

No., Name, Rank & Regiment 104312 Hazleton W. A.

has been examined as to his fitness as Pilot

and found
- fit as P. Pilot
- unfit in any capacity as flying officer.
- temporarily unfit.

His acuteness of vision is as follows :—

V.R. without glasses 6/6 With + 2 lens Blur

V.L. without glasses 6/6 With + 2 lens

Remarks :—

Signed H. R. C. Capt

For Presdt. Aviation Candidates Medical Board.

Date 8 JUL 1918

No candidate is allowed to fly without having this form in his possession. No duplicate will be issued.

Certificate of passing health exam

Cadet classmates

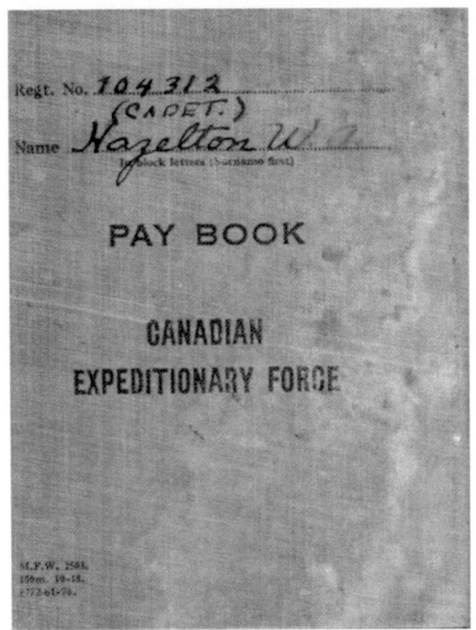

Regt. No. 104312
(CADET.)
Name Hazelton W. A.
In block letters (Surname first)

PAY BOOK

CANADIAN
EXPEDITIONARY FORCE

Front of paybook

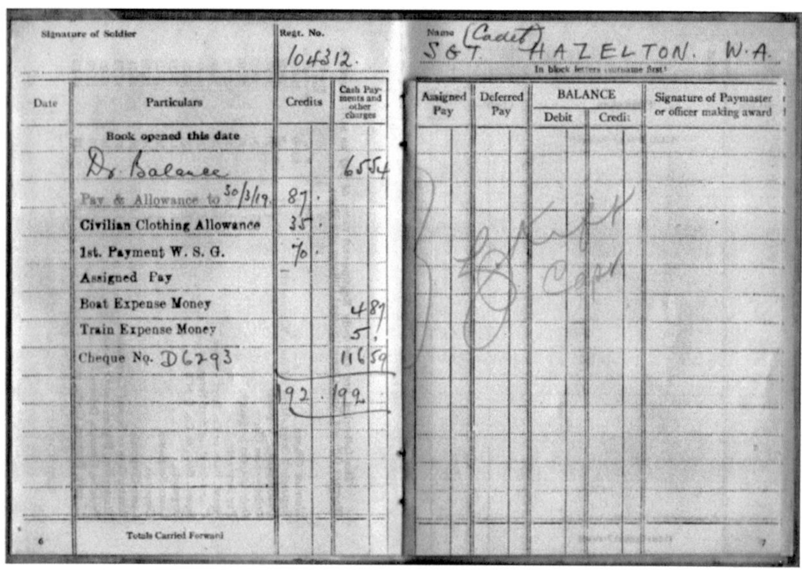

Signature of Soldier

Regt. No. 104312.

Date	Particulars	Credits	Cash Payments and other charges
	Book opened this date		
	Dr. Balance		65.54
	Pay & Allowance to 30/3/19.	87.	
	Civilian Clothing Allowance	35.	
	1st. Payment W. S. G.	70.	
	Assigned Pay		
	Boat Expense Money		4.87
	Train Expense Money		5.
	Cheque No. D6293		116.59
		192.	192.
6	Totals Carried Forward		

Name (Cadet) SGT. HAZELTON. W.A.
In block letters (surname first)

Assigned Pay	Deferred Pay	BALANCE		Signature of Paymaster or officer making award
		Debit	Credit	
				Capt

7

Pay book details

F.S. Form 751.

Copy of Air Ministry Weekly Order 409 of 3rd April, 1919.

FLIGHT CADETS AND CADETS, R.A.F.—OUTFIT GRANTS.

(This Order does not apply to Overseas Cadets who are being repatriated.)

1. Flight Cadets who graduated "B," or who qualified as observers, before 31st December, 1918, and have not been commissioned, will be granted an outfit allowance of £38 10s., to be applied in payment of outfit bills already incurred, any balance being payable direct to the flight cadet.

2. All other flight cadets will be granted compensation in respect of sums expended in the purchase of outfit before the date of this Order up to a limit of £23 10s.

3. Cadets will be granted similar compensation up to a limit of £35.

4. The grants in paragraphs 1 and 2 will in each case be additional to any outfit which has been provided in kind, or to any payment up to £11 10s. made by the General Services Pay Officer under Air Ministry Order 74/1919, in respect of the purchase of flight cadet's outfit.

5. Personnel affected by this Order should immediately render claims on the form overleaf to Messrs. Cox's Shipping Agency, 110, St. Martin's Lane, W.C. 2, supported by bills for the expenditure incurred. *(Claims should not be sent to the Air Ministry.)*

6. The opportunity will be taken of honouring, as far as possible, any "chits" on Messrs. Cox and Co. given by flight cadets and cadets when outfit was purchased. If any "chits" are outstanding, in respect of which the flight cadet or cadet concerned fails to send in bills, he will be notified by the Shipping Agency of the manner in which it is proposed to apply the grant.

7. (*a*) If the bills have *all* been paid (and subject to no "chits" being outstanding), the full amount of the bills within the appropriate limits of paragraphs 1, 2 or 3 above will be refunded direct to the cadet.

(*b*) If *none* of the bills have been paid (including outstanding "chits"), they will be paid (by Messrs. Cox) within the limit of the appropriate grant by direct remittances to the outfitters on the cadet's behalf in order of priority of date.

(*c*) If *some* of the bills have been paid while others are unpaid, the unpaid bills (including outstanding "chits") will be paid as in paragraph 7 (*b*), and the balance (if any) of the grant will be remitted to the cadet, within the limit of the amount represented by the receipted bills.

8. Flight cadets eligible under paragraph 1 for the full allowance of £38 10s., regardless of whether or not they have expended that amount, need not send any *receipted* bills. Any balance of the grant, after the unpaid bills (and "chits") have been paid, will be remitted direct to the flight cadet by Messrs. Cox's Shipping Agency.

9. The only articles which will be regarded as "outfit" for the purpose of the allowances, under paragraphs 2 and 3 above, are as follows:—

2 Pairs Ankle Boots (or 1 pair Ankle Boots and 1 pair Knee Boots).
3 Shirts.
3 Pairs Socks.
14 Collars.
1 Pair Gloves.
1 Tie.
1 Pair Puttees.
2 Jackets.
1 Pair Trousers.
1 Pair Pantaloons or an additional Pair of Trousers.
1 British Warm.
1 Waterproof Coat.
1 Cap and Badge.
1 Camp Kit.
1 Trench Coat.
1 Cardigan.
1 Haversack.

Cadet Clothing Allowances

Junior Army & Navy Stores.

PRICE LIST FOR "R.A.F." OUTFIT.

	£	s.	d.
Tunic Complete, Best quality Whipcord or Barathea, £6/6/- and	~~5~~	~~16~~	~~6~~
Slacks	2	8	0
Bedford Cord Breeches	3	3	0
R.A.F. Cap and Badge	1	3	0
2 Shirts, 2 Collars and Tie	1	6	9
Trench Coat	5	5	0
Fox's Puttees		9	0
	£19	9	3

Outfits splendidly Tailored, faultlessly cut, and absolutely correct in every detail.

For Terms apply at

5, West Hill, St. Leonards-on-Sea,
Near Palace Pier,
Open DAILY, 9 - 8 p.m.

AND

15, Claremont, Hastings,
Open MONDAY, WEDNESDAY and FRIDAY,
9 30 a.m - 8 p.m.

Also Branches at . .
Bexhill, Reading, Oxford, Bath, Bristol, Denham.

Price list for cadet uniforms

Promotions, Appointments, Reductions and other Casualties affecting the

DAILY RATE OF PAY

Date Effective	Nature of Casualty	Part II Order	Unit.	Signature.
5.12.17	Prom to rank of Actg L/CPL	325	M.R.D.	Extracted from old A.S.P.B
7.9.18	Prom Actg SGT. for Cadet Course	353 19.12.18	M.R.D.	

Note:—Fines and forfeitures are not to be entered on this page; they will appear in column for Cash Payments only, on pages 7 to 14.

Pay book

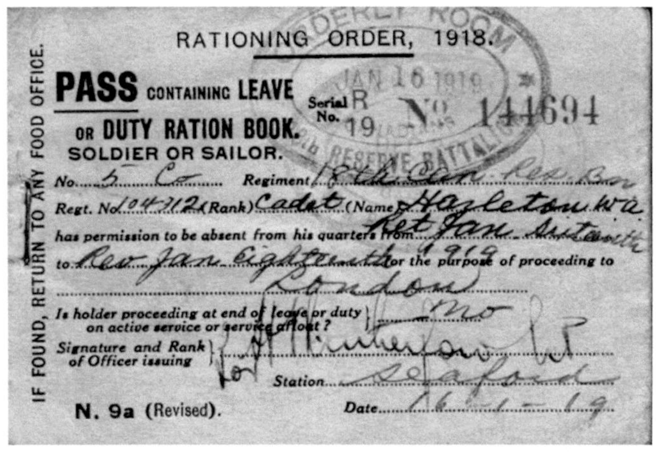

IF FOUND, RETURN TO ANY FOOD OFFICE.

RATIONING ORDER, 1918.

PASS CONTAINING **LEAVE** OR **DUTY RATION BOOK.**

SOLDIER OR SAILOR.

Serial No. R 19 No 144694

No. 5 Co. Regiment 18th Can. Res. Bn

Regt. No. 1043112 (Rank) Cadet (Name) Hazleton W.A.

has permission to be absent from his quarters from Rev Jan Sixteenth

to Rev Jan Eighteenth 1919 for the purpose of proceeding to London

Is holder proceeding at end of leave or duty on active service or service afloat? No

Signature and Rank of Officer issuing [illegible] Lt for Lt

Station Seaford

N. 9a (Revised). Date 16-1-19

Ration book

Chapter Eight
Homeward Bound

Just three weeks after the previous letter was written the Armistice was signed and the war in the western front suddenly stopped. There were millions of men under-arms who now had to be demobilized. But how was this to be managed and how long would it take? Not only did the men have to be disarmed but all of the materials of war had to be managed. The soldiers couldn't just lay down their rifles and walk away from their cannons and tanks.

There also had to be a plan for getting each soldier back home. For all of the B.E.F. soldiers this would involve a boat ride and probably then a train ride to their home. For the Canadians, the boat ride would take many days and how many could be put on each ship and how many ships could be scheduled?

To get the soldiers completely disengaged also meant arranging their pay until they were returned to civilian life. This had to include advance pay to allow them to take local transportation once off the ships.

This whole effort had to be a monumental undertaking so it's no wonder that it took months before Walter was able to actually return home. In the meantime he and his fellow cadets had to sit around and make do the best they could. This wasn't going to be easy for them.

No 2 S. of A., R.A.F.

PER ARDUA AD ASTRA

EXETER COLLEGE,
OXFORD.

Nov. 20th -18.

Dear Folks:

Well I guess you are wondering what I am doing now since the Armistice was signed. Well we have stopped work and the worst of it was, Instruction ceased on our last day of the Course, so we had no finals. If we had been a couple days ahead we would be carrying on and would be Qualified before returning. But I happened to be unlucky

Received ma-ma's fine letter OK. Always Address c/o Cable.

etc. while there for everyone is still rationed.

No·2 S·M·A·, R·A·F·
Nov·20th, 1918

Dear Folks:

Well, I guess you are wondering what I am doing now since the Armistice was signed· Well, we have stopped work and worst of it was Instruction ceased on the last day of our course so we had no finals· If we had been a couple days ahead we would be carrying on and would be Qualified before returning· But I happened to be unlucky this time· We are merely putting in time until further orders are issued· We have no idea what will be done with us·

But the War is really and truly over so we are not worrying a great deal about the rest· It is over and I am still alive so ought to be mighty thankful· <u>But</u> naturally everyone turns to their own future now, and wonder what will happen· We are just waiting indefinitely· Coal is so scarce we have none in our room, and it is very cold now· So we have to get out and go wherever we can· It costs too much money but we have no choice· I have spent a lot of money on the attempt for a Commission and will not get it after all I don't suppose, so will not get the expected increase in Pay and it costs over twice as much to get along as an Officer Cadet as it did in the Infantry· But it is worth it· I have learned an awful lot in the past few months and do not regret the expenditure excepting that I had to ask you for it· I could not have got along without the money cousin Arthur sent at all· I wanted you to use my Assigned Pay but little thought I would have to ask for it again· But I am sure you understand how anxious I was to get into something worthwhile and all for a couple of days I would certainly have succeeded· They may yet decide to give us a chance and I will take it if it <u>does</u> not mean to stay over here too <u>long</u>· I don't expect to be back in under 6 months for it will take a long time to demobilize and in that time I may be able *to get far enough into this work to give me a good start in that line after the War. If not I will have to wait until I return and look around for a job I can take a real interest in.*

I expect a good long leave sometime around Xmas and New Years so will be with Cecile. I certainly do not expect any Xmas parcels this year and instead of attempting to send any I would much rather you would enclose what you can in a P.O. to Uxbridge for me. A leave costs a lot of money and I must buy my rations etc. while there, for everyone is still rationed. This leave may be indefinite pending return to Canada, and we must take it and make the best of it. It will probably be the last one in Eng. too. Under these conditions which popped up so unexpectedly I wish I could borrow a few more pounds from someone. But there is no use of me attempting to as I know no one. If you can see your way clear I wish you would do it for me. If not, well I will have to take chances on doing what I can.

You see I did not receive the $25 you sent and have not been able to locate it. Have you tried? I hope you will not think I am trying to get too far beyond my means. Things may turn out better than I expect. On discharge the Gov. will certainly make a pretty good allowance and if we get our "Flight Cadetship" it will be more.

It is going to be hard to say such an indefinite "Goodbye" to Cecile, but must be done, goodness knows how long for. She will feel it I know, but will not say much for she understands perfectly how things stand.

Well the "Flu" is still pretty bad here but is declining fast. I hope the new move proves satisfactory.[39] *How is everything?*

[39]His parents had just moved back to Hayward, Wis. after the war was over.

Did you receive the photos? They are undoubtedly the last in uniform.

I heard from Ruth not long ago, but not from Helen, But I can hardly expect to when I write as I did.

You had better keep this letter and I will write to them separately as I have more time now. I am not feeling too well just now but probably on account of cold. Heaps of love to all and Wishing all the Happiness Xmases & Merriment of New Years.

I am always your loving son,

Walter

P.S. Please excuse scrawl. I am writing under difficulties. It is crowded in here. (Y.M.C.A.)

(Received Ma Mas fine letter OK. (Always Address c/o Cecile)

Just that suddenly the war was over and it couldn't have been at a worse time for the cadets. They were just days away of the final exams that, when passed, would qualify them for actual flight training and a corresponding pay increase. The conditions they were left with were dire in England with shortages of all the essentials and severe rationing. Prices of everything had increased over the past two years so even though they might be able to travel around, the cost of doing so would be steep.

On the good side Walter was expecting to be able to visit Cecile for quite a while. However, this was going to cost a lot of money and without the expected pay increase it was going to be difficult. The fact that the cadets were expected to live and carry on as officers had already been putting a strain on their expenses so Walter had been asking for money from home but not receiving it yet. He was wondering if assigning some of his pay all through his time with the B.E.F. was a mistake because now he is in need of it and didn't want to ask for some to be sent to him. And the process of getting the money took time if it got there at all.

At this point Walter is still hoping that they will allow him, and his fellow cadets, to complete the exams and get their promotions. Even if he doesn't, he is glad to have made the change to get into the R.A.F. training. It has cost money but he thinks the training will benefit him once he gets back to civilian life.

Also, now that the war is over and all the troops are to be sent back home the reality of how he and Cecile would pursue their engagement had become critical. He would have to return to Canada on one of the troop ships and leave Cecile behind until they could make arrangements for her to join him. However, Walter seems to think, at this time at least, that this was something they could work out. She and her family had to be concerned about this but still hopeful they all could come to Canada. Life in England was really tough at this time with all the shortages so the prospect of getting away from it all had to be very desirable.

*****

Now that Walter had a lot of free time he would catch up on his writing. His letter home was just one week later:

PER ARDUA AD ASTRA

Exeter College,
No 2 S. of A., R.A.F.,
Oxford.

Nov. 27th. 1918.

Dear Folks:

Your letters have been coming thick and fast this week or so. Two from Ma Ma (Nov. 5th.) (Oct. 31st) and Papa's (Oct. 29th) Another from Ruth posted Nov. 5th., Believe me I appreciate them to. I have more time than I know what to do with, at present so am writing to all I can.

I like to hear from the girls too. I can plainly see Gladys is getting along pretty good. Her writing and her letters improve

and many died before

of our spare time.

at Xmas, it will take

you have rented it

Exeter College
No·2 S· of A· R·A·F·
Oxford
Nov· 27th, 1918

Dear Folks:

Your letters have been coming thick and fast this week or so· Two from Ma Ma (Nov 4th) (Oct· 31st) and Papa's (Oct· 29th)· Another from Ruth posted Nov· 5th· Believe me, I appreciate them too· I have more time than I know what to do with at present so am writing to all I can·

I like to hear from the girls too· I can plainly see that Gladys is getting along pretty good· Her writing and her letters improve noticeable (six) each time· It is too bad school had to close but I hope it has re-opened by this time· Is the Flu abating yet? There seems to be very few cases of it here at present· I presume the cold weather setting in helped to keep it down· As far as masks go I have seen no one wearing masks, but here they were worn in parts of London·

The school here provided large basins of gargle "Candy's Fluid" and it seemed to help a lot· There were very few cases among the Cadets· All windows were kept open regardless of colds and we all kept out doors as much as possible· We all have hard colds but not much flu· "Ammoniated Quinine" was used very extensively I believe in some cases· The Doctors here are so scarce people had to proactively do without them, and in many cases caused sickness from improper use of medicine· Schools etc· were closed· All public places were put out of bounds to all Cadets for a couple of weeks, only· Went to <u>picture</u> shows etc· At one time Oxford had the highest death rate of Eng· Yes, pneumonia set in in some cases and many died before they could obtain Med· assistance·

Coal is so scarce we are not allowed fires in our rooms so naturally find places where there are fires. Our Cadets Club & Y.M.C.A. are crowded all the time. You see there are lots of Imperial Officer Cadets here too.

We expect a move of some kind very shortly now, as they want to start the Colleges again. Perhaps it will be leave, we are all hoping so anyway.

Although a great many are anxious to get discharged and clear of the service, there are many who wish to continue this course and obtain some kind of Qualification while they are at it. And I am one of them. If possible I mean to get "Pilot's Wings" before I leave the Air Force. We may be commissioned and may not be. Every one of us are anxious to know what they intend to do with us and are certainly "fed up" with merely putting in time. I have been thru the best parts of town, and have been canoeing on the Thames which flows thru here. Everything is very pretty and must be marvelously beautiful in the summer time. It is really too cold to take advantage of our spare time. It is funny how a fellow gets tired of putting in time even though he is in one of the most Beautiful places in Eng. But I am anxious to get busy and do some things and not merely waste time. I believe Canadians are returning every day now. I wonder if I will have the option of going via New York. If they return me to the place I enlisted, and that place only, well, I can see Helen and the other friends before going to the States. Is it much out of the way to return to the States from Canada, via New York, or rather Brooklyn? I do want to see all I can, and as many of the folks as I can while I am on the go. But as you know, I am far from familiar with the U.S. railways, etc. But that won't worry me if they give me enough money to carry on with. It is possible they will return us to our former rank & unit, but not likely after we have had all this training. It would hardly be fair and besides it has cost us so much for the outfits & general expenses.

Believe me, they are fierce in spite of all you can do. We are expected to do everything much too stylish for my liking, especially on Privates pay. If I get the Month's leave at Xmas it will take some extra from somewhere. If they pay us our Board and room allowance it will not be so bad.

I know you folks will understand why I cannot send the presents I wish to, don't you? However I expect to spend my leave all at Uxbridge. It will be too expensive and well nigh impossible to travel much. I would like to see Derrick & Mrs. Walker before leaving Eng. but unless they give us some leave or time in Liverpool before sailing it will be unlikely.

We are all anxious to hear about the "Wonderful Day" over there. A Pal of Mine here has just received a letter from Toronto written Nov. 12. They evidently went wild too. My but it is great to think it has really ended and we have done what we knew we would do with God's help. I am proud to wear Canada on my shoulder too. Am enclosing a clipping perhaps you have not seen. Personally, I did not do much to win the War but I did what I could. I wish I could have got to France in time to see the finish at least, from the Air. What an experience it has been for those of us whom God was Gracious enough to spare, and may He justly reward the fellows who gave all to Gain this Wonderful Victory.

I know you will find a great Difference in me. I am far from what I would be. But have been, Oh! so miserably weak in many ways. God has been so good to me and my prayers have been that I may be of some real benefit to the World. My experience in the past three years has been wonderful and will probably help me in many ways.

I sincerely hope your latest move to Hayward will prove to be a good one. So Papa is in the Army, well, well. In Uniform? But it is over now. Practice is sure to be good, is it not?

You ought to have that P.O. for $25.00 back by this time. Hastings P.O. & Lloyds Banks say they have no record of it, but that it would be returned after 2 months.

Papa spoke of enclosing a receipt but must have forgotten it.

I had a fine letter from Ruthie. Yes, I certainly think she needs Red Cross Discipline. She would like it too. But of course that will change now.

I am glad you are keeping the place at Exeland[40] for me. But hope it will not be too expensive. I will undoubtedly be glad to settle down on it until I look around. I am glad you have rented it for 1919.

I did not want you to depend on me too much. At present I am keenly interested in Aerial Work and if there is a good opportunity would certainly take it there in the U.S. But I cannot say anything definite until I know something definite as to the R.A.F. & Canadian Gov's plans regarding Cadets of the Air Force.

About that parcel, if you sent it with my Rank and Number c/o Cecile it ought to be alright I think. Thanks so much. But I wish you would not bother about a parcel this year. It isn't really necessary is it? But it is probably too late to say so now. But believe me, I appreciate it. I love to get your nice long letters telling me all about things, too. Ma Ma's clippings are certainly interesting. More than I enjoy reading them.

I am so sorry for poor Helen & Jack. It is too bad. I do hope they will soon pick up. I certainly would not like to farm in Canada.

---

[40]Exeland is a town in northern Wisconsin

Well, I have been writing this all morning. Au Revoir. I wish I could be with you for Xmas but my thoughts will be.

A Merry Xmas & Happy New Year to all.

Forever

Your Loving & Trusting

Walter

With nothing else to do now that all the training has stopped, Walter is catching up on his letter writing to his parents and sisters. Also, the letters from home are finally coming through so his thoughts about what he will do when he gets back are becoming more intense. He is still hoping that the R.A.F. will allow them to finish their training and get their "Pilot's Wings" and the pay increase that would go with it. He doesn't seem to be in a hurry to get home if getting his wings is possible.

But he is also thinking about what to do when he gets there and thanks his father for keeping a farm in northern Wisconsin that he could take over. However, later in the letter he comments on how hard it has been for his sister, Helen, and her husband to make a living by farming. They had stayed behind in Canada after they were married in 1916 and were trying to keep the farm going. Walter had mentioned his concern for how they were doing in several of his letters. It is no wonder that he says that he would not like to farm in Canada.

The conditions at the school they were housed in seemed pretty stark. The scarcity of coal must have been very rough on them, especially combined with the sickness that was rampant. But he was able to tour the town of Exeter and was very impressed with it.

He doesn't say much about Cecile in this letter but the relationship is holding up well despite his not being able to visit much during this period.

*****

Then two weeks later he sends another long letter while still at Exeter. He is expecting a long leave and looking forward to spending the holidays with Cecile and her family:

PER ARDUA AD ASTRA

No 2 School of Aeronautics
Exeter Squadron,
R.A.F. Oxford.
Dec. 10th-18.

My Dear Father Mother
And Sisters:

I presume this will reach you about Xmas, at the rate mail goes now. I am awfully sorry that the cards I am getting are late. But not very late. There are so many friends that I want to send one to this Xmas.

Things are slowly getting ready for the Happy Season here. It will be a happy one this year too, for some. It will be very hard on

wish to go over. If I

to visit New York or not.

No. 2 School of Aeronautics
Exeter Squadron
R.A.F. Oxford
Dec. 10th, 1918

My Dear Father Mother and Sisters:

I presume this will reach you about Xmas at the rate mail goes now. I am awfully sorry that the cards I am getting are late. But not very late. There are so many friends that I want to send one to this Xmas.

Things are slowly getting ready for the Happy Season here. It will be a happy one this year too, for some. It will be very hard on the many families who will have faces missing.

I will undoubtedly be at Uxbridge with Cecile by that time. We expect a nice long leave next week. Perhaps we will be Commissioned after all. The Canadian Authorities are trying to fix us up. Undoubtedly, we will come out on top.

Thanks so much for the Xmas parcel. Cecile says it has arrived so I told her to keep it until I come up; she will enjoy it with me. Oh, yes, I was up there last week for a couple of days to see Cecile's father. He was warned for a draft to France and I guess expects to go this week. It is rather too bad, for if he goes he will not be home for Xmas. I wanted to see him, for I will probably be home before he comes back again. I managed to get Special leave for the Purpose. I had a good talk with him and he thinks I am doing right by not being married before my return. It is understood that I go back alone and look around. If I decide on the farm alright. I will have to decide upon the time for Cecile to come.

Mr. & Mrs. R....... want to go over if I can let them know there will be something to do as soon as they get there. He thinks he would like farm work. Mrs. R. as you know is a trained nurse and thinks she ought to be able to get something to do. Does English Qualification hold good over there? However, she wishes to be somewhere the other side of the water if Cecile is. She may change her mind yet, but at present I am at sea as to what to do. It is quite a proposition. Cecile is certainly coming over, sooner or later, even if I must wait until I can come over for her. If I had the money, even though things are as indefinite as they are, I would get married before I go back. It will be awfully hard to say good-bye so indefinitely, but of course I would have to do that anyway. It would be impossible to go back together. However we are still waiting for definite word as to what is going to happen and cannot say anything until then. We may be back in a month or so and maybe in 6 months. I have no idea as to whether I will be able to visit New York or not. But certainly wish to see the Wadsworths.

Say, have you received my Photos yet. So you think Cecile looks rather tired, do you? Well, most of her photos are like that but I think it is a fine one of her. I am sorry you did not receive the one of Cecile and her mother. They were both rather sober, but otherwise fairly good. Oh well, I will show them all to you before long.

I don't think there will be very much trouble with Germany now. It is Over.

I feel awfully sorry for poor Helen & Jack. It is too bad. I do hope they will get along alright.

Has the Flu abated yet? How is Papa? Things are going pretty well here. Lots of excitement over the Election[41].

I am sending some news of Oxford which I believe will be of General Interest.

---

[41]Woodrow Wilson had just been re-elected.

Did you trace the $25? I do wish I had it for Xmas.

I must do a lot of writing in the next few days sending Xmas cards, etc.

I must go to bed now, it is "Lights Out". Wishing you and all the Best of Everything for Xmas and a most Happy 1919 with more Love than I can begin to express. I am always Your Loving & Trusting

Walter XXXXX

P.S. Cecile wishes you all the same as I do.

Having been cooped up at Exeter all this time Walter has been able to get away briefly to go to Uxbridge to talk to Cecile's father about their plans. Even though Walter would have liked to get married right away he didn't have the money to do so and Cecile's father was happy that was the case. He had probably seen a lot of situations where youngsters got married during the war and then later have to deal with their husband being killed in combat, leaving them alone.

Cecile's father wasn't opposed to the marriage itself and was actually looking forward to the possibility of he, and his wife coming over, once Cecile and Walter were married in the U.S. or Canada. But, they all were struggling with how Walter and Cecile were going to get together once Walter returned home. Was Walter going to come back for her, which would cost a lot of money, or was he just going to send for her?

This was going to be a critical discussion while he was visiting during the holidays.

*****

The authorities did grant the leave Walter was hoping for so he was able to go to Uxbridge for the holidays. He would write his next letter from Cecile's home:

what are the addresses of the Wadsworths?

10 Cowley Mill Rd,
Uxbridge Mdx,
England.
Dec. 28th 1918.

Dear Folks:

Well here I am at Uxbridge. My Leave is up on the 2nd. unless extended after that I do not think it will be long before we will be on our way home. But nothing definite. The Can. Authorities seem to have all they can do without troubling about R.A.F. cadets. I do wish they would tell us something so we could plan a little.

I received Mother's nice long letter, written Dec. 5th, a few days ago. I told you the sweater, cake, and gum arrived O.K. did I not? They were all lovely. The sweater is fine. It would have been the very thing for flying, but of course that is out of reach now, I am afraid. Only 2 more

appreciate it too. I was going

10 Cowley Mill Rd.
Uxbridge Mdx
England
Dec 28th, 1918

Dear Folks:

Well, here I am at Uxbridge. My leave is up on the 2nd unless extended after that. I do not think it will be long before we will be on our way home. But nothing definite. The Can. Authorities seem to have all they can do without troubling about R.A.F. Cadets. I do wish they would tell us something so we could plan a little.

I received Mother's nice long letter written Dec. 5th a few days ago. I told you the sweater, cake, and gum arrived O.K. did I not? They were all lovely. The sweater is fine. It would have been the very thing for flying, but of course that is out of reach now I am afraid. Only 2 more days, I would have been flying now. But oh, well I am going back to the Country soon now. I will decide then about the best course of action. It is impossible to be married before I return now, even though I want to so much. It would take more money than I could begin to get ahold of in the first place. But I think Cecile will be over there before so very long anyway. You see it would be impossible for us to go back together if we were married. It could not be arranged now, so we have decided upon the only open course.

I cannot see why Qu'Appelle H.S.[42] could credit me with anything at all for I only got part 1 of the 3rd you know? And my Work at Oxford could in no way effect Med. Training. It was merely Aeronautics and a short & hurried Course at that. No, it seems impractical to think of Medicine or Surgery now. It would take much too long and although I know nothing about it, it doesn't

[42]Qu'Allelle is the school he had been attending before signing up

seem to appeal very strongly. I'll find something I will like before I am there long. Perhaps the farm if it is still available.

England is at present quite excited about Wilson. London is overcrowded.

I am awfully short of money now and don't know what I will do. Owing to some misunderstanding at Can. Head Quarters they did not pay us the back Sgt's pay from the time our training commenced which we should have got. They expect us to live like Officers on Privates' pay.

It will be alright to send Cecile the Journal because she will undoubtedly be here another year. They certainly appreciate it too. I was going to subscribe for it myself for her, but find I cannot very well.

I have had a letter from Helen. They seem to be having a terrible time of it. I wonder what the outcome will be.

I had the Clipping about Jack Hamblin some time before your letter came from his Mother. He has certainly done fine. I feel rather ashamed of myself all this time in Eng.

Well, Cecile is waiting for me now. She sends her love to all. I hope you are all enjoying the Xmas & New Year.

Tons of Love to all from, Your Loving

Walter

P.S. Have just received Papa's welcome and interesting letter; will write again soon.

What are the addresses of the Wadsworths?

Four months go by since the Armistice and Walter has finally gotten back to Canada. There are no letters to tell what has been happening during that time. Walter and Cecile had not gotten married before he left but undoubtedly had spent a lot of time together since there was no more training being offered by the authorities. Nevertheless, Walter was very happy to get back to Canada and to be able to visit his friends and relatives:

77 Walmer Road,
Toronto, Ont.
(Good Old Canada)
Mar. 28th 1919.

Dear Folks:

Well at last I am here in Canada. We arrived on the "Royal George" at Halifax on Tues., and finaly reached Toronto last night. It took no more than ten minutes to get everything fixed up and now lo and behold I am a free man. It hardly seems creditable, but yes I have my discharge in my pocket. I called up Secord and of course I came out home with him. They want me to stay as long as possible but I have decided after finding yours, and several of Cousin A. W's letters at the G. D., to go over to New York and see them and then home. I am not going West, after all. I want to get home first. When they said they would give me a ticket to any destination in U.S. or Canada I took Hayward quick

77 Walmer Road
Toronto, Ont.
(Good Old Canada)
Mar. 28th, 1919

Dear Folks:

Well, at last I am here in Canada. We arrived on the "Royal George" at Halifax on Tues. and finally reached Toronto last night. It took no more than ten minutes to get everything fixed up and now, lo and behold, I am a free man. It hardly seems creditable but yes I have my discharge in my pocket.

I called up Secord and of course I came out home with him. They want me to stay as long as possible but I have decided after finding yours, and several of cousins A.W's, letters at the G. D. to go over to New York and see them and then home. I am not going West after all. I want to get home first. When they said they would give me a ticket to any destination in U.S. or Canada, I took Hayward quick.

The Wadsworths seem anxious to see me so I will get a ticket there and return here. Then I can come to Hayward on my free warrant. Frank's brother who used to work in the Railway Office says he thinks he can fix me up with a stopover at Chicago if I wish it, so I will have an opportunity of seeing uncle Willie's, will I not? Do they live at Joliet? If you write to me in care of Cousin Arthur it will probably find me there. Of course I am not sure of how long I will be there yet but will let you know. I am sure to be home in about 3 weeks as far as I see now, perhaps sooner.

I would liked to have gone to Regina to see all of my old acquaintances but perhaps that will come later. Home is my attraction now.

How is everybody? Well, I hope.

Thank you for the affidavit. It may be useful. But I don't think there will be any trouble. They have given me authority to enter U.S. in uniform upon leave or discharge within 30 days so that will be O.K.

Cousin Arthur has sent me their addresses so I will go down there on Mon. next (Mar. 31)

Write won't you. I am going to wait and get my civvies at home or would you advise me to get them here in Toronto or New York?

Well, I must write to them now. Au Revoir for not very long. With lots of love.

Your Affectionate

Walter

Back in "Good Old Canada!" Walter has returned at last and is anxious to visit his friends and get back home to find a job. There is no mention of plans to bring Cecile over as he is just trying to figure out what he is going to be doing for a job. He is also wondering about his education since he had not finished high school before he enlisted over three years ago.

This is to certify

that Hazelton W. A.

served at the following Ground Schools, as a Cadet of the Royal Air Force in 1918.

Cadet Brigade.	Passed Examination. ~~Did not complete course.~~
No. 2 School of Aeronautics.	~~Passed Examination.~~ Did ~~not~~ complete course. (NO EXAM. GIVEN)
Armament School.	~~Passed Examination.~~ ~~Did not complete course.~~

And has now been ~~demobilised~~ returned to his unit on account of the cessation of Hostilities before he had an opportunity of receiving instruction in aviation.

W. A. Robinson

Secretary of the Air Council.

Date: 13. 12. 18

Certification of passing R.A.F. exams

War Service Badge
Class "A" No. A 133807

CANADIAN EXPEDITIONARY FORCE

DISCHARGE CERTIFICATE

THIS IS TO CERTIFY that No. 1043?7 (Rank) Cadet

Name (in full) Hazelton Walter Arthur enlisted in

the 68th Battalion

CANADIAN EXPEDITIONARY FORCE at Regina, Sask on the first

day of September 1916

HE served in 52nd Canadians and Royal Air Force

and is now discharged from the service by reason of Demobilization. ~~Medical Unfitness.~~

THE DESCRIPTION OF THIS SOLDIER on the DATE below is as follows:—

Age 21

Height 5 ft 10 in

Complexion

Eyes blue

Hair

Marks or Scars mole – left elbow – mole – abdomen, right

W. A. Hazelton [illegible]
Signature of Soldier

[illegible signature]
Issuing Officer
For Lt
O.C. No. 2 District Depot.
Rank

Date of Discharge

No. 2 DISTRICT DEPOT
MAR 27 1919
TORONTO

Date MAR 27 1919 19

N.B.—As no duplicate of this Certificate will be issued, any person finding same is requested to forward it in an unstamped envelope to the Secretary, Militia Council, Ottawa, Canada.

M.F.B. 39.
1049-D.P.-300M-11-18.
H.Q. 1772-39-882.

Discharge Certificate

Returning Home On the Royal George

Cunard Bulletin.

Saturday, March 22nd, 1919. "ROYAL GEORGE."

LATEST NEWS

Received from the Marconi Wireless Station at Washington, U.S.A.

SURRENDER OF GERMAN MERCANTILE FLEET DELAYED.

Berlin.—Despatches from Berlin state that the surrender of the German Mercantile fleet will be somewhat delayed on account of the present serious shortage of bunker coal. The shortage is due partly to strikes and to the immense transportation difficulties.

TRAGIC DEATH OF MRS. DUDLEY ASTOR.

NON-BOLSHEVIK FORCES DEFEATED.

London.—The Non-Bolshevik forces having been defeated by Soviet forces, have retired towards Odessa from the North, according to a Moscow despatch.

REVOLUTION AGAINST SOVIET GOVERNMENT.

London.—There are unconfirmed reports that a revolution of the moderate element of the social democratic party against the Soviet Government has broken out in Petrograd, according to a German wireless report.

U.S. LOAN FOR CHILIAN RAILROADS.

Santiago, Chili.—The newspapers here assert that a loan of eighty-nine million pesos is being raised in U.S. for Chilian railroads.

FORMER AUSTRIAN EMPEROR SEEKS RESIDENCE IN SWITZERLAND.

Geneva.—The Swiss Government has received a

Chapter Nine
Moving On

His next letter is just one week later from New York City while visiting at uncle Wadsworth's home. Clearly Walter is working hard on finding a job and has pretty much given up on the farming idea. He has repeatedly mentioned his concern about the difficulties his aunt, Helen, and her husband, have been having with their farm. This must have turned him off on the farming idea. Again in this letter there is no mention of Cecile but they surely have been communicating by letter and trying to figure out how and when she would come over.

Walter Wadsworth's Office
104 Worth St.,
New York City.
Apr. 2nd.

Dear Folks:

Well here I am in New York, with the Boys. I arrived yesterday morning. Have seen them all but Doc. Emory and will probably see him today. I stayed with Walter last night. They are going to give me a fine time, I know.

I will go back to Toronto in a week and will probably start for home about the 12th. My ticket says C.P.R. but I want to go via Chicago if possible. You see my free warrant is from Toronto so I must go from there.

I dont know how things

Walter Wadsworth's Office
104 Worth St.
New York City
Apr. 2nd

Dear Folks:

Well, here I am in New York with the Boys[43]. I arrived yesterday morning. Have seen them all but Doc. Emery and will probably see him today. I stayed with Walter[44] last night. They are going to give me a fine time I know.

I will go back to Toronto in a week and will probably start for home about the 12th. My ticket says C.P.R.[45] but I want to go via Chicago if possible. You see my free warrant is from Toronto so I must go from there.

I am very glad I came to see the Boys and New York. It is liable to be a valuable trip to me. I am sorry I cannot get out west to see Helen & Jack but it does not seem practical now. I must be in civilian clothes by the 27th you see.

How are things? I am getting anxious to see you all.

As yet I cannot decide upon the farm or anything

else, but I am trying a line on some Business Work.

Frank Secord's father has been in Newspaper and Advertizing business for a long time and is handling an advertising campaign thru Canada and the U.S. for the Great War Veterans Association and wants returned men to send out. He will give me an idea of the work and a chance to try it when I return to Toronto. It will be a paying job while it lasts this summer. Then there is a Press trip to Battlefields of Europe I can get in on with Frank if I wish

---

43The "Boys" are his uncle Wadsworth's sons.
44Walter Wadsworth
45Canadian Pacific Railroad.

too, and like the work. But I want a long talk with you before I make a Decision. I don't know how things are with you folks yet.

Well, I hope this finds you all well and happy.

Lovingly,

Your son,

Walter

P.S. The Boys all send their best Regards

Some place this is Believe me.

Walter has been having a wonderful time visiting with relatives in New York City but is also struggling with finding a job. The idea of farming is again mentioned as well as a summer job for veterans doing some advertising in Canada.

*****

The first pages of the following letter are missing but probably was written several months later.

4.

WISCONSIN TELEPHONE COMPANY
~~OPERATORS REST ROOMS~~
RACINE

It means a lot to
a fellow if he can
stick to one town &
get aquainted, &
establish a good
reputation, I can see
that now.
I mean to get
education with my
work. Others have
done it, & I can too.
I am getting along
fine with I.C.S. &
can switch my
work to anything
I want with them
without extra fees
excepting the differences

entirely
After I get into H. S.

It means a lot to a fellow if he can stick to one town & get acquainted & establish a good reputation. I can see that now.

I mean to get education with my work. Others have done it & I can too. I am getting along fine with I. C. S & can switch my work to any line I want with them without extra fees excepting the differences in the price of course. I can't say I would like the idea of going to Ashland especially as the College is in the Country. I would not be satisfied to put all my time in general studies. I want to get all I can in whatever line I am working in and I will study overtime for the rest. That course of reading on Psychology is worth a pile. It shows that memory training etc. must be developed on the same system as "Roth's Memory Course" took up. If you are not using it I wish you could send them down to me.

I realize you are doing all you can to give me an opportunity of getting started right and appreciate it. But at the same time I feel I am following the best course open to me & pray for Guidance.

I had a fine time in Illinois. Uncle Willie & Ernest met me at Symerton Xmas night in Ernest's Dodge. The next Day we saw George Beckwith & all Family & had Dinner there. Then we went to Arthur Jones' for Supper & spent the Evening at George Johnston's place.

The next day we went to Walter Johnston's for Dinner but he was away & I only saw him a minute or so.

(Another page seems to be missing)

This course may be changed at anytime & they will start me at the beginning of the new course. If the new one costs more, of course, I must pay the difference. I think I can get along on the money I will get here pretty soon. But can save nothing. I can see marriage is still out of the question.

After I get into H. S. (missing pages)

Yes, I like my work & am making the most of my spare time. I want to finish this course if possible. It is well worth it.

There are lots of Socialists in Racine but the Mayor has prohibited any meetings of a Bolshevik nature & so headed them off in the first attempt.

Anna has Floyd Gibbons' "And They Thought We Wouldn't Fight". She will bring it back alright. So never mind my old Bible. I have my Testament O. K.

That picture of Ruthie may be in the bookcase or upper part of the desk. Or look in my uniform pockets.

I was talking to Jack Glover again, & he says since a lot failed on Thanksgiving exams there is plenty of room in the U. at Madison and they are putting on an adults course which does not require H. S. Graduation. I don't know any other details yet. What do you think of it? When does the Ged semester start? He says Sumonson & Shocky Moberg intend to come down after Xmas too, and the bunch of us could room together. But I am interested here and like the work. The I. C. S. course is well worth finishing and I would like to stay until I do. If I did not manage to get work to help get thru it would be pretty expensive I am afraid. Are you sure you could spare the cash?

Say, this fellow "Pollick", Mrs. Smiley's nephew, who is working here too, is an old friend of Frank Bentley's too. So is Smiley.

I enjoy Smiley's game "Landball" very much. We get on the Gym floor a couple times a week.

I am enclosing Last Sunday's Church Programme. It will give you an idea.

Well, I am going to ring off for this time. When do you expect Jack?

Hoping everybody is well & happy. With love to all

Affectionately,

Walter

P.S. Thanks for addresses

Walter is trying hard to get a better education but the cost of doing so makes him ask for more money from home. This also makes him realize that marriage is still out of the question for the time being. At this point, at least he is still committed to bringing Cecile over but hasn't got enough money to do so.

He has been going to a local church and found it very interesting and has enclosed the programme from the previous Sunday. His religious upbringing seems to have been re-ignited.

****

Almost a year goes by until the next letter. He has been staying at a local Y.M.C.A. but has finally found a line of work that suits him:

Y.M.C.A.
Racine Wisc.
Mar. 15th 1920.

Dear Folks:

Mothers letter arrived this morning. Goodness but you are having a siege of trouble this Winter. Is it still cold up there? The snow is about gone and it is like Spring today. But oh so changeable, it may be freezing tomorrow. I managed to get another dandy cold last week. This climate is giving my catarrh an awfully good hold. Have you any good "dope" for catarrh?

It is OK about the employment Agent

Y. M. C. A.

Racine, Wisc.

Mar. 15th, 1920

Dear Folks:

Mother's letter arrived this morning. Goodness but you are having a siege of trouble this Winter. Is it still cold up there? The snow is about gone and it is like spring today. But oh so changeable; it may be freezing tomorrow.

I managed to get another dandy cold last week. This climate is giving my catarrh an awfully good hold. Have you any good "dope" for catarrh?

It is OK about the underwear. I am glad you did make some use of them. I don't need them now anyway. My work is not going to be as greasy as it has been.

I am in the 2nd week of "Case Plow Co's" Salesman's & Service Course. I like it fine & feel I am in the right line at last to make a start. They have excellent Professors as Instructors and we take up the details of all of their Implements including Wallace Tractor. My farming knowledge & Agricultural Course is of value to me in lots of ways now. Case's have an excellent line of Implements & have the proof of it with them. I am deeply interested and it is awakening a new interest in Agricultural development in me. I had some difficulty in getting into this "Course" but my Aviation & Hoit Parr Experience helped me immensely. The man in charge of this Branch, Mr. Mueller, was Chief Engineer of the Curtis factory. The Employment Agent "Mc Folare" used to work out of Regina for Hoit Parr Company. He knows "Gaylord" & "Weizlet," remember them?

I expect they will send me to some Branch House in the Spring. I have no idea where but I would like to keep Racine as Home Headquarters.

Had splendid sermon yesterday. They are having Sermons every night for 3 weeks & boosting (?). They turned on and dedicated a new Electric Cross on top of Church last night. 8 ft high & it revolves, flashing a beam like a light house. It can be seen clear down Main St. and far out on Lake Michigan. The Church is jammed every Sunday, twice a day.

I must close now. Hope Jack is well again & Gladys. Tell Ruthie I will write but am awfully busy.

Tons of love to all from

Yours Truly

Am enclosing Bulletin & card they are distributing. They have a half page in "Daily" street car ads. Revolving Cross church every night and a wonderful minister besides a clean cut upright boosting brotherhood of Members. The Congregations have doubled & more since Hargett came here. Did you see the piece in Country Gentlemen about him?

Walter seems to have found a line of work that he is uniquely qualified for, having spent his formative years on a farm. Operating tractors was almost second nature and his R.A.F. training on engines probably helped as well.

More significant in this letter are his comments about the church he has been attending. In particular a preacher named I. M. Hargett who has recently arrived and is captivating a local congregation. Walter's religious background has been aroused by this preacher and he has written Cecile in order to get her to understand his beliefs. He has been back in the states for about a year during which he and Cecile have been communicating by letter. Walter has been trying to "sell" Cecile on the evangelistic message this preacher has been offering but apparently without much success. This has added to Cecile's concerns about being truly accepted by Walter's parents and especially his father who was, after all, an educated man and practicing doctor.

****

Three months later Walter writes again about his concerns with the engagement to Cecile and his worry about a split:

ELECTRIC LIGHTED HOT AND COLD RUNNING WATER STEAM HEATED

ESTABLISHED 1856

The Hotel Constans

C. W. CONSTANS, Proprietor

Blue Earth, Minn., June 4 1920

Dear Folks:

Well I have been pretty well on the go the last two weeks. I was at Fulda last Thurs. & Fri. & saw Chants. Of course they were very much surprised when I told them who I was. They seem to be very well liked in Fulda which is by the way a town of about Haywards size or perhaps a little larger. I had Dinner with them, but there time is taken up with so many little things, we did not have much time to visit. A Circus "Yankee Robinson's" was there while I was,

(Titan & "Uncle Bus Trucks")

The Hotel Constaus
Blue Earth, Minn
June 4, 1920

Dear Folks:

Well, I have been pretty well on the go the last two weeks. I was at Fulda last Thurs. & Fri. & saw Chants. Of course, they were very much surprised when I told them who I was. They seem to be very well liked in Fulda which is, by the way, a town about Haywards size or perhaps a little larger. I had dinner with them, but their time is taken up with so many little things, we did not have much time to visit. A Circus "Yankie Robinson's" was there while I was and our Dealer there had one of our Tractors on display in it. Quite an unusual Ad.

Did you know Mrs. Switzer. Died not long after Mr. Switzer. Ethel told me all about it. Both are buried in Vancouver where they had been on account of Mrs. S. health. Gus & Ethel plan on going there to settle the Estate.

Well, last Sat. I put on a Demonstration in plowing at St. Peter. We had the "Oil Pull", "Twin City", "Samson" & "Fordson" there and left them so far behind in quality of work, speed, power, and ease in maneuvering that they could say nothing.

. (Titan & Hart Parr backed out.)

There were about 60 wealthy farmers there to witness it. The Twin City wanted to show her power in sod so we went into a pasture and did so. She had long extension lugs and we had spare lugs. We were put on our plows down about nine inches & walked along faster on low than she could on high. Our plows were so deep they could not scour but hers scoured nicely, but could not go under five inches without stalling the tractor. Well, we sold our outfit then & there on the farm with certain prospects of many more this year. It happened that this was an unadvertised demonstration of seemingly minor importance so Goodyear nor any other celebrities were present. So I pulled it single-handed with our territory Salesman from Mankato to witness. Those boys could not do enough for me after that. It feels awfully good to know you can trim them all, believe me. Well, I went to Mpls. Sat. night & spent Decoration Day there. A large number of Canadian War Veterans were there, including a number of R.A.F. pilots. Well, we all paraded in a unit and were received with plenty of applause. You undoubtedly read an account of the big parade, did you not? I met fellows there I had not seen since we returned from overseas. It was sure good to fall in once more & march to the Bag Pipers who played us along the march. It was some Mpls. Pipe Band.

Well, I went to Comfrey Minn. Tues. to fix up a 3 wheeler & came on Blue Earth Wed. Yesterday I drove to Bricelyn & Elmore with our dealer here and gave the driver of the County Road Machine here a few points. Today I return to Comfrey to finish a job there. I hope to be in town Sat. night. I usually manage it that way.

I am worried very much about Cissie. I had the letter you forwarded OK. She does not understand the change in me. I only wish I could let her hear a man like Hargett a few times. She keeps saying she is not good enough and all that and we both plainly see that a gulf is coming between us. Unless I can make her understand & see things differently there will surely be a break. She doesn't seem to care as she used to. I don't blame her for her religious views as I know why they are that way and how she has been brought up. Oh well, I am trying to think up a strong letter to write, & pray for guidance in doing it. If the poor kid could only see that what I am trying to do will do more for our future happiness than anything else, but she misunderstands & there is no one there to help her see things in their true light.

Please don't let the Girls read this part of my letter. They won't understand.

Well, how is poor Jack coming? And Ma Ma & Helen & all?

I haven't heard from any of you for an awfully long time.

Had a letter from Ruth last week.

Let me know all about everything.

God Bless you all,

Heaps of Love,

Your Affectionate, Walter

Walter had found a strong religious resurgence and was trying to convince Cecile about it. Her background seemed to be too far apart both religiously as well as socially/economically. Having been away for England for over a year Walter senses that Cecile had become more distant and not able to accept his religious beliefs Walter tried to convince Cecile that they could come together on these issues and they probably exchanged a number of letters trying to work this out.

Nevertheless the breakup occurred within a couple months. It would have been interesting to see some of the letters that were going back and forth during this time. We can only speculate that they must have been very emotional since these two seemed very much in love just one year earlier. Walter had been concerned about these differences right from the beginning of the relationship but was sure they could work things out over time. With Walter's deeply religious childhood and its resurgence after getting back from England the gulf with Cecile turned out to be too difficult to surmount. Cecile seemed convinced that she was not going to be fully accepted by his family and that she couldn't accept his strong religious beliefs which had been reignited when he got back home.

For Cecile there was also the frightening thought of traveling alone by boat to the U.S. She had never traveled more than a few hundred miles before so thinking about such a trip would have been a big concern, Also there was the uncertainty of what would happen when she first arrived. Would Walter actually been at the dock when she got off the boat?

Their love wasn't strong enough to overcome all these issues. The distance and length of time apart only accentuated the problems despite Walter's effort to make it work. So Cecile gave up of the idea of coming to America at all. Walter considered returning to England to attempt to heal the rift but that wasn't practical or economically feasible. Thus this wonderful romance came to a sad ending.

The End

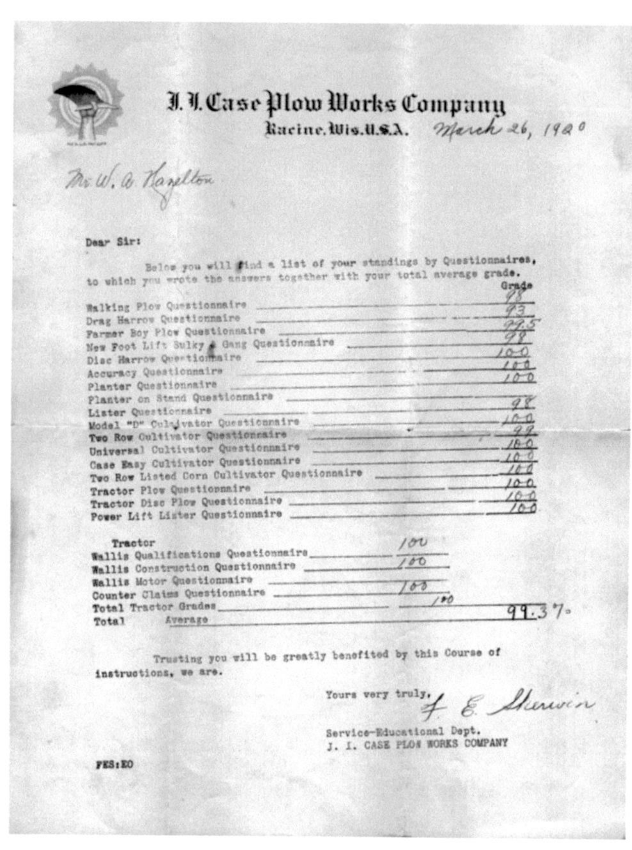

J. I. Case Plow Works Company
Racine, Wis. U.S.A. *March 26, 1920*

Mr W. A. Hazelton

Dear Sir:

Below you will find a list of your standings by Questionnaires, to which you wrote the answers together with your total average grade.

	Grade
Walking Plow Questionnaire	98
Drag Harrow Questionnaire	93
Farmer Boy Plow Questionnaire	99.5
New Foot Lift Sulky & Gang Questionnaire	98
Disc Harrow Questionnaire	100
Accuracy Questionnaire	100
Planter Questionnaire	100
Planter on Stand Questionnaire	
Lister Questionnaire	98
Model "D" Cultivator Questionnaire	100
Two Row Cultivator Questionnaire	99
Universal Cultivator Questionnaire	100
Case Easy Cultivator Questionnaire	100
Two Row Listed Corn Cultivator Questionnaire	100
Tractor Plow Questionnaire	100
Tractor Disc Plow Questionnaire	100
Power Lift Lister Questionnaire	100

Tractor		
Wallis Qualifications Questionnaire	100	
Wallis Construction Questionnaire	100	
Wallis Motor Questionnaire		
Counter Claims Questionnaire	100	
Total Tractor Grades	100	
Total Average		99.3%

Trusting you will be greatly benefited by this Course of instructions, we are.

Yours very truly,
F. E. Sherwin
Service-Educational Dept.
J. I. CASE PLOW WORKS COMPANY

FES:EO

Plowing Competition Score Sheet

First Methodist Church

Corner Main and Eighth Streets

Bulletin Vol. X. Racine, Wis., Mar. 21, 1920 No. 29

EVANGELISTIC SERVICES TO-DAY TO EASTER

Every Night at 7:30

Can God and your Pastor count upon you?

1—To Boost them?

2—To attend them?

3—To Pray for them?

4—To try to win one to Christ?

Jesus said—"Follow me and I will **make you** Fishers of Men." That means you and me.

The Friendly Church for Friendly Folks

I. M. Hargett, Pastor, Res. 932 Lake Ave. 'Phone 3693

Musical Director, Mr. Russell Lewis. Organist, Miss Amy Lewis

Take this Bulletin home for reference or to give a friend.

I. M. HARGETT

At the Church of the Revolving Cross

"Up or Down WHICH?

Cor. 8th and Main

CHORUS CHOIR

PIPE ORGAN

ORCHESTRA

EVERY NIGHT

(Over)

Church Flyer

Epilogue

Walter had to deal with a number of adversities during his early life. Growing up on a desolate farm wasn't that bad but his ordeals in the trenches in France and Belgium were a rude awakening. Another setback was the termination of his pilot's training when the war suddenly ended. He had worked hard on the training and spent a fair amount of money on uniforms only to see it all was to no avail. And then, after he returned home from Europe, the breakup with his fiancee must have been crushing. But Walter was determined to move past these set-backs.

His first job back in the United States was selling and servicing tractors for which he was uniquely qualified. His early farm experience using tractors and then his training in the R.A.F. about the mechanics of motors served him well. He seemed to enjoy this work but soon he began using his ability with machines to get into the sale of typewriters and other office equipment. He eventually became a branch manager of an Underwood Office Equipment store in Rochester, NY and later owned his own store in Elmira, NY.

When Walter enlisted in the Canadian armed forces in 1915 he automatically lost his U.S. citizenship. Now that he and his parents were residing back in the U.S. he applied for and was subsequently repatriated in 1924.

The R.A.F. pilot training had whetted his appetite for flying so, after a few years back in the U.S., Walter continued with flight training. He got his pilot's license and enjoyed flying as a hobby.

A couple years after the breakup with his English fiancee Walter met a beautiful Norwegian girl named Ilia Gunders. They were married in 1924 and had four children. They lived happily together for over fifty years.

When World War II broke out Walter decided to enlist in the Army Air Force and was granted a rank of Captain based on his previous pilot training. The Air Force was eager to sign up people like Walter who had previous flying experience even if they were 45 years old.

After some training in the U.S. he was given the position as a Commanding Officer of the 456th Sub-Depot of the 100th Heavy Bombardment Group near Diss, County of Norfolk, England. He was in charge of the repairs of the heavy bombers when they returned from their missions.

Walter's health problems did not recur. He died at the age of 77.

Dr. Hazelton in his office

Walter with his flying buddies after the war

Bibliography

Cassar, George H. *Hell In Flanders Field,* Dundurn Press, Toronto, 2010

Marshall, S.L.A, *World War I*, Houghton Mifflin Company, Boston . New York, 2001

Nicholson, G. W. L. *Canadian Expeditionary Force 1914-1919*, McGill-Queen's University Press, Montreal & Kingston, 2015

Burg, David F. and Purcell, L. Edward, *Almanac of World War I*, Press of Kentucky, 1998

Conversations with the Historical Society of Regina, Saskatchewan, 2019

Printed by Libri Plureos GmbH in Hamburg,
Germany

9 798893 957075